Ovens and Apricots

A story of inspiration
for single parents

KATERINA SCOTT

BALBOA.PRESS

A DIVISION OF HAY HOUSE

Balboa Press books may be ordered through booksellers or by contacting:

Balboa Press
A Division of Hay House
1663 Liberty Drive
Bloomington, IN 47403
www.balboapress.com.au
AU TFN: 1 800 844 925 (Toll Free inside Australia)
AU Local: 0283 107 086 (+61 2 8310 7086 from outside Australia)

Print information available on the last page.

ISBN: 978-1-5043-2325-3 (sc)
ISBN: 978-1-5043-2326-0 (e)

Balboa Press rev. date: 11/23/2020

Contents

Introduction

I was booked on the Lockerbie flight 103 December 21, 1988. The Pan Am flight that was blown up as it took off north out of London. It was a regular flight that originated in Frankfurt, Germany, via London Heathrow and New York City JFK, final destination, Detroit, Michigan. It was known as the first terrorist attack by air and there were no survivors. I was booked on the London to New York transatlantic leg. I changed my flight. I still have the itinerary with it crossed out in pen. That was a lucky day for me age 21. My journey of life did not end that day. There are no guarantees in this world but let me tell you a second chance at life is worth the journey.

I have to say I am not a great reader, never have been, managed to somehow pass English Literature with credits in school only reading the first and last pages of any given chapter and based my essays on the back cover of the book. I am still unsure how that is possible, other than I could write well about something I had not read. However, give me a law textbook and I cannot put it down. I am very unsure about that too, as with most things in my life!

I see so many books 'based on a true story'. I have always been in awe of the based on aspect. This book is based on a true story for sure, infact, to clarify that, this book is a true story. True in every aspect of the word, some parts I still find hard to believe but yes it all happened!

Let me give you a brief insight into the beginnings of this idea. I am now at the other end of this 30 year part of my story, starting writing on my laptop in a tiny kitchen sitting at a centre bench with my laptop propped up on a chopping board as I do not have enough room in this apartment for a desk.

I am wearing my favourite Kmart black jumper, blue striped pyjama shorts, and slippers I managed to find at a discount shop for $4.99. My apartment is a studio hence not a lot of room, decked out with pictures of the 4 children I raised for the most part alone, who are now all grown up and have left home, many plants, well possibly too many, but, the oxygen level in here must be spot on! It is affordable rent which you will start to understand throughout my story, that I do not have a material asset to save myself, apart from my $1,300 car which ran alright, apart from being towed off the highway last weekend because it overheated and was about to blow up, and I have just sold it to the wreckers for $300…zero assets now…did not end up running alright.

However, this story digs a lot deeper. The 4 babies that I brought into this world are my assets, assets which far outway any material item or monetary value put on anything. You will join me on a whirlwind of life as a parent, relationships that I am not even sure why I went into them and the humorous satire of survival.

Prologue

I think deep down that every little girl has dreams of her knight in shining armour coming in on a horse and marrying her and they live happily ever after. My little girl dream ended up in the form of the movie 'The Man from Snowy River'[1]. When I was about 14 this movie was produced and I saved my pocket money and went to see it, fell instantly in love with the lead actor Tom Burlinson and decided I would marry him…or somebody resembling a country boy with a stock hat and drysabone coat, maybe a horse, I was only 14 so was perhaps a little confused.

Funnily enough I became friends with one such boy when I was about 16. He was a year older and had his drivers licence. He was a jackaroo, which, in Australia is a farm hand. This boy was terribly good looking and we went to some black tie balls together. I kissed him once at a party down the river in an apple shed, he came to help me up after a silly boy threw a barbeque chicken that managed to hit me in the head and knocked me over. It was my introduction to B & S ball type parties where everybody would be dressed up yet have to walk through mud to get to these parties in sheds on farms and by the end of the night you ended up smelling of a combination of mud, sheep manure and Bundaberg rum. Very Australian.

Ironically, he and I became great friends and used to be part of a small group of friends all the same age, getting drivers licences, going to pubs underage, but back in those days no one ever seemed to ask why we were all only 17 yet drinking and dancing in public bars. Our parents liked our friends so none of them minded either, or knew in some such cases! Well, let's be honest, they were all having barbeques and dinners with the same parents and were just happy we were all having fun! It was the 80's, none of this discriminatory, security conscious rubbish that our children have to contend with these days. We were all free, no phones, no internet, if

---

[1] *The Man from Snowy River,* Cambridge Productions, Edgley International & Snowy River Investment Trust Pty Ltd, (1982).

you wanted to see a friend you just rode your bike to their house and often ended up having coffees or wines with their parents and your friend was not even home.

So my Man from Snowy River was my best male friend. We did so much together. We were 'mates'. We used to go out together, sit in the pub together, I never felt I had to dress up around him, we would just catch up and talk about all sorts of stuff. Everyone thought we were a couple, which suited us as we could just have fun without people asking us out! We never kissed again. It was just a fabulous friendship. There were days I would wake up in the morning at my parent's suburban home and my mother would say that he was asleep on the front lawn in his swag after he had been out with the boys. There were times I would come home and he was in the kitchen talking and laughing with my mother or out at the barbeque talking to my father having a beer. Half the time I was not even there and he would have visited. And I used to do the same with his grandmother. I remember driving to their house and showing her my first car and going to his other grandmother's house and drinking tea listening to stories about the war.

He fixed the headlight I smashed on my car while I was crying. We went to the B & S farm parties together in his ute singing to Jimmy Barnes and I would sleep next to him in his ute and we were never intimate, he used to just protect me. He had a new jackaroo job and wanted to cook me a roast dinner, that was quite funny, it was burnt, but we had this whole big house to ourselves in the country and just sat up talking in his bed eating chocolate. We laughed so much. We both had little 'flings' with other people but my favourite time was just us, no pressure, laughing about how we broke up with them! He went to live at his uncle's farm in a cottage and there was another jackaroo. He wanted me to move in so I took the third room. The cottage was so cold that your electric blanket would steam. The other jackaroo was a bit of a wild boy and used to grow marijuana in the shower. I had a fling with him along the way while my Man from Snowy River had a fling with a girl I had gone to school with. We used to use the fence palings for kindling for the cottage to get the fire going at night, and then one day his uncle said after winter had gone.. and so had the fence, that he was sure there used to be a fence there. We just said no, there was never a fence.

And then we parted ways. He left for the outback to be a jackaroo in the outback on a large cattle station where they would muster stock by locating them by helicopter. I went overseas to live. My Aunt and Uncle were there so it was an opportunity to travel and live abroad.

I think that my Man from Snowy River mate was my ideal husband idea, baring in mind I was still only 19 years old and terribly immature and was still infatuated with Tom Burlinson…

He wrote letters to me from the cattle station and I wrote from overseas and gradually time went on and we stopped writing. We were young and adventurous. I told him he should put himself through Agricultural College with some money he had received from his father and that was the last time we really talked. I went to London then back to Australia. My Man from Snowy River had gone. We did not have the phones and Instagram or Facebook accounts to keep in touch with friends back then so basically, you did not see them if they went away, unless you turned up at their parent's house at some point to find out where they were or they had arrived home so you saw them then!

You are about to embark on my journey, a journey that half the time I do not understand how I managed to hold myself together, but a journey that I was destined to live, one filled with so much laughter, so many fun times, tears, hardship, all rolled into one.

The point of sharing this journey is to make you laugh, to focus on the silver lining in life and to show you that somewhere, in all the difficult times, we can still muster the courage to keep on keeping on, to keep our dreams alive, and that NOTHING is too difficult to overcome. I had to learn the gift of laughter, it totally saved me, and; in amongst this journey of ups and downs, I would not change any obstacle on this path that I was clearly designated to endure.

I chose to follow my own heart, to not stay in places where things were not working, and things do have a strange way of working out as they are supposed to. I do not believe that divorce is entirely negative for children and their environment, in some rare cases it can actually make them stronger as people, such as mine, because my little babies survived a dreadful parental divorce and that in itself is not something that anybody plans or wishes on their children.

So this book is aimed at adults, single parents, people in good and bad relationships and people in abusive relationships and also young adults with parents going through hard times. It is a reflection on life really. You need to lift your mood above what is going on in your life and while trying to find an answer, laugh and enjoy the adventure along the way.

Every person faces some form of challenge throughout life, it is how you deal with that challenge that counts. I remember my father used to always say that through adversity you will find the seed to greater opportunity. And trust me, when you fumble your way through my story you will realise that I was at times wishing for not just a small seed to greater opportunity but more like a pineapple sized one!

So let me begin, with my first wedding…

Chapter 1

My first wedding

So every good story has to start with a funny beginning, well, maybe funny, when you are only 23 years old and have no actual idea why you decided to marry your friend's older brother, 6 years older, when the only thing you seem to have had in common was you both liked pumpkin soup and Bundaberg Rum, and your friend had a wedding dress so you decided that was a good idea… to get one of those…

Such deep feelings…of course all of my friends were still in the University Bar on Wednesday nights while I was facing playing settled girl in stable relationship, very questionable, on a farm, in a cottage with no heating, rats running across the beams at night and on a bright night you could see the stars from the bed, on the inside of the house through the iron roof that had no lining, just the iron, with possums having their own Olympic Games up and down the roof all night, the odd one sliding off as the ice settled on the iron outside and you would hear the thud as the poor little critter hit the lawn and ran off.

The cottage had a large verandah overlooking a very pretty river, which was lovely to sit on for about 1 month of the 12 months of the year as normally it was without sun and absolutely freezing cold. Then the sheep would often be on the verandah or running through the white sheets you would have hung on the wire clothes line that disappeared into the paddock over a rock wall…or, on a lucky day (not) there may be a bull staring at you on the verandah or eating the new lettuces you had planted to try impressing your soon to be mother-in- law…yes that one person you just wanted to hang on the clothesline next to the sheets, upside down…

So we went south to my prospective parents-in-law's home for the weekend and there was no actual proposal…a vague mention from my future husband that soon we would marry, a

1

few months back. Every girl's dream was your future mother-in- law coming towards you in the kitchen with a ring box as you looked stunned thinking only of hanging her upside down on the clothesline and; knowing her fashion sense of wearing red with pink at the same time, that dreaded thought of some disastrous piece in the box that you were expected to love and wear forever....suddenly the wedding dress idea had felt somewhat fuzzy, to say the least, but I was unfortunately trapped between her, my future husband and the dishwasher with no real way out...

And there it was...great aunties ring, so worn it had cracked, quite pretty apart from one stone missing right in the middle...with my future mother-in-law telling me the diamonds were not very good quality but it will do for a daughter-in-law because no one will ever be good enough for her son. I have to say it was not really like those beautiful romantic movie proposals, I would have at least thought my future husband might have at least asked..instead of my future mother-in-Law... so, as a result, I was engaged to the family, not him. Needless to say this was the beginning of my 'fairytale' marriage...

My parents lived north on the coast at the time, the wonderful coastline that I now call home and I spoke to my mother and said that we should be married there, rather than on the island, where I was raised. Naturally this opened a can of worms with their family as it was all so inconvenient and my future mother-in-law lost her realm of control for that time...nothing short of interesting...she took on the job of doing the flowers for the wedding...so in essence we ended up with very non tropical type flowers in glasses on the tables that strangely resembled weeds. Normally she was very artistic with flowers, however, that was on the island, a totally different climate.

Everyone travelled a few months later to the Coast for the wedding. My sister was still at school and my Bridesmaid. I had asked my two best friends who both let me down, even though I had worn a large pink dress that made me look nothing short of a meringue wearing a large pink bow in my hair for one of their weddings... The professional makeup for her wedding started itching as I walked up the aisle and I was the one drenching my face in the hotel bathroom scraping if off with paper towels to only look like a pink meringue with a face like beetroot because I was allergic to it. But that was okay...she still let me down when it was my turn....

"T'was the night before the wedding, when all through the house, not a creature was stirring"...just my grandmother and great aunt drinking copious amounts of whiskey, my grandmother asking if I was sure I was doing the right thing, my great aunt telling me to not paint my fingernails and to do something with my hair. My sister was too young to really understand and was unsure why I made her carry a dried flower hoop up the aisle that I had not chosen either, my brother busy trying to look like Hugh Grant with his haircut and keeping his car going… Mum held the fort drinking wine and Dad told me the cars were free with the restaurant… classic.

So I coloured my hair darker because my future husband liked blondes, and; in particular the blondes on Baywatch television series…in particular, Pamela Anderson, that had to be a sign…at 23 what do you really understand about signs anyway? I had the cream raw silk dress that cost me $1000 and made me look like a cream meringue…well at least I was the right colour, very 1990…with a top that resembled the late Princess Diana's dresses…very 1990 as well. I looked at it hanging in the spare room with the terrible cliché dried flower halo I was to wear while I pretended to my great aunt that we had not been living together…

And then; after enough wine and my grandmother pouring whiskey into me telling me I will need it with that family, I stood up and told everybody at dinner that I did not want to be married yet.

Silence….

My great aunt said that she had flown from the city, classic guilt trip. My mother just about choked on her dinner and sculled the rest of her wine. Dad said the cars he had booked were paid for….and that we should just do it as it was all booked and non-refundable…and…. that we could sort the rest out later…Of course, it was 1990 so there was no texting messages or anything like that so my husband to be, poor fellow, had no idea, that I had decided I did not want to be married, the night before what was supposed to be the 'best day of my life'.

Is it not amazing the path life takes you, the decisions you make, the ones you do not make and the adventures, disasters, wonderful moments that it brings…this was undoubtably one of those.

"Good morning Nanny", I had said sharing a bedroom with my grandmother that gallant eve of my wedding.. she had cramp from drinking too much whiskey so was lying with her legs in the air in her classic floral pyjamas…

And there I was getting ready for the supposed magical day of my life. I had stared in the mirror wondering what I had decided to do, and why I did not look more like Julia Roberts… I put my meringue dress on and had to wear a terrible brooch my future Mother-in-Law gave me, a gold moon…who wants to wear a gold moon to anyone's wedding.. let alone your own… but I put it on in any case to keep them happy. My shoes I had had covered in the same material as my dress..equally discusting and very uncomfortable. I had a hangover so my mother gave me concealer for my eyes….great start…thinking back, I think my mother looked the best out of all of us as she had only drunk wine not the whiskey….but we all had champagne before the car arrived which helped the hangover, even though my mother was telling my father off for ordering the car too early…but that was him…always early… to everything… flights, functions, everything.. and this was no exception…

So my father and I made it to the Vintage cars…naturally it was as windy as anything on the road up the coast to the church, my father was in a rush to get there, I think, deep down, he was just hoping that I might actually stay married after this day… My veil blew off up the highway and my father was climbing over the backseat trying to retrieve it before it became stuck in the back wheels. The driver could not hear us for the wind so there was no way we could stop. We both started laughing… and we arrived early at the church and there was nobody there. So we did a trip around the block and literally hid in behind the front seats of the car so nobody could see us sitting down the road. It could not have become any worse…my dream wedding?? Maybe NOT!!

Finally we made the big arrival…my uncle was taking photos and being genuinely annoying. We walked up the aisle of a huge church…with 32 guests…of course my father had to say, to wave to all the people on our way..I walked to the cliché wedding march, had not even thought of a song that meant anything, probably because nothing with him really meant anything, I do not think I had ever felt more confused in my whole life, what was I doing?? Oh well too late now, I was halfway down the aisle with my grandmother glaring at me because she knew I was unsure….

Unsure…a word that was to change the life of a 23 year old and terribly immature young adult….

So I was married. The reception was interesting; my husband smoking like a chimney at the table as everybody did in those days, while I drank all the wine I could get my hands on…. and that is about all I have to say about that day.

And that was it.. the beginning of a most rewarding yet difficult story… 30 years of my life. The point of this journey is to make other men and women laugh, hope, accept, challenge, gain strength and believe that there is a light at the end of any tunnel in life and the ability to accommodate many disasters is what makes us whole.

After a week on the Coast, where my parents lived, we returned to the farm, and as the plane descended onto the island I looked out the window at the grey clouds and cows in paddocks thinking is this it?? We arrived at the farm and, notably the cottage was freezing cold and there was no food in the fridge. Of course there was no wood because my husband had not thought of that…which became a regular occurrence over the next years of my life. It was a cold September and the river below was flooded as normal on the island at that time of the year, which, of course meant we had to locate firewood on the the side of the river that did not seem to have as much as we could not get across.

So, here I was, married to one of the wealthiest families on the island whereby you actually have no claim to any of it and they seemed to love watching us living on basically nothing but a small wage below the poverty line with my husband's trade. I was working part time and commuted, which was only 20 minutes, and life went on.

We went to the large family Christmas up at "The Big House", a 52 room calendar house with an elevator, which, back in 1990 was rare, and I was the new bride on show to all the cousins while they all stared at me judgingly. Fortunately I had grown up learning to ride horses with some of them and I had attended a prestigious educational facility so I was classed accordingly as the same. It felt like I was a cow in a cattle show, nothing short…except I did not leave with a ribbon.

I set up the house and sewed cushions to try to brighten the cottage up as it was very dark inside with small windows and no sun coming in. I was surrounded by all my husband's belongings and the entire cottage looked like his house he had had on the other side of the country, when I had flown over there to see if this relationship was going to work the year before…at 22…even worse …even younger… and even, at the time, more immature than myself the 23 year old bride. I only had my antique chest full of special bits and pieces as I had been traveling the world and had never accumulated any furniture.

I remember liking the top floor of the cottage, apart from the rats on the beams, and; the possums looking at you through the holes in the roof at night but the top was painted white and had bigger windows and exposed beams, quite quaint in January as with no roof lining it was warm, totally different in winter …

So, while at home I baked cakes and made soup and did all the 'wifey' type projects to impress being married to this family… I planted vegetables, which were mostly eaten by possums or when the sheep decided to push the gate open, I used to go walking to collect kindling and wood to keep warm. My husband worked long hours in field service as a mechanic so it was generally me, a movie and glass of wine trying to keep the stupid fire going! My friends would call and ask me to go into town to lunch or dinner etc but it was all too difficult as I was now running a little farmhouse and with all that entailed keeping the sheep from wearing our sheets down to the river or trying to keep the dog away from the work dogs when on heat.. My life had changed.

In terms of accepting my new life, I used to walk for miles out across the river. It was peaceful. I barely saw my friends anymore. Of course we saw his friends all the time as they were married couples all older than me and I would dread being judged by them as I cooked and slaved in the kitchen watching them all laughing and drinking. But I would have my own little party over the stove and have my wine while I cooked… alone. Oh great, I had become the cook.. I never thought marriage would be this lonely. I felt more alone than when I had been single. There was just more work to do. His friends were different. I like to think I am a normal person. This lady was very judging, it did not help I was thinner than her as that was an instant fail at any form of friendship on her part, even though I made her an apple crumble at a dinner party to try to be friends...she still disliked me... I really am not sure why, I was nice to her. I never sat on their toilet though, maybe she picked up on me wiping my knife and fork before eating at their house?! So back then 28–30 year olds seemed so different to me at 23, unless I was more immature than I envisaged.

Chapter 2

24 and not feeling well…

Well…this was new…in amongst juggling a job, bulls, cattle, floods, sheep, possums, rats, different friends, constant dinner parties because I would cook for everybody, the Autumn set in at the farm. Autumn on the island can be long beautifully sunny days lingering with daylight savings and endless sunsets over the mountains… or…it suddenly turns into the Antarctic it seems and you reach for every conceivable rug on the couch or bed, every jumper you every had and Ugg boots…

This Autumn was no exception of the latter. Firewood…there was no wood…as usual, as I watched my husband leave for work so I went walking into the bush that morning to retrieve some logs, dragging them by hand up the hill from near the river so I did not freeze for the day, laying them on the verandah, getting the axe, to try, in my best not so practical way to cut them up. Even the dog and cat sat looking at me blankly!

I felt somewhat out of breath walking up the hill but thought it was just the weather and maybe I was getting a cold. My jeans felt a little tight. They had felt like that on the weekend as I went to my husband's work dinner and preceded to drink 12 rum and cokes thinking I was going to get fat like my husband's friend's wife.. the one who did not like me….Oh is that what happens when you marry? You make apple crumble for guests and do not even eat it but put on weight because you are married?? Gallant thoughts of a 24 year old…

So I thought I would call my mother. "Are you pregnant?" Her first question…oh dear… She told me to go to the Doctor.

And there it was…a baby inside me. Deep down I had always wanted to be a mother, my utmost dream infact. I told my husband and naturally the family were all excited and I was distinctly told I should produce the first grandson for the next generation….pressure….?! They did not actually care for a healthy bouncing baby of any gene, just the boy…it was all I heard about..

Meanwhile, I felt dreadful, whoever this little being inside me was, it was growing rapidly, I was out of most of my clothes at 6 weeks. I felt dreadful. Could not stand the smell of meat cooking, lettuce in the fridge, well that had to go!! All I wanted was beer and pizza. I used to cry for pizza….Naturally, I only had a sip of a shandy at times and didn't drink beer being pregnant.

My sister-in-law had had a miscarriage so my mother-in-law preceded to tell me every day that I would have one too as she wanted her daughter to bear a child before me as we were the same age. I never saw sense in that…or anything she ever really said actually. So I distanced myself as much as I could in those months…until the "Kitchen Tea Party"…oh dear …

My mother in law organised the event, I had no say (of course) as to who was to attend this inaugural occasion set on the farm of my sister-in-law, who, had become pregnant as well, a few months behind me but long enough for the entire occasion to be all about her and half of the guests were her friends not mine, infact I had not met a few of them.

So I went home feeling like a moose as now quite a large baby was growing inside me, with many useless gifts and smocked dresses for a boy or a girl…?! And knitted booties with rose buds hand sewed on them, very cleverly sewed and gorgeous had it been about 1940…

This baby kept growing….and growing…. I finally finished work as I was too big to wear any decent work clothes and we could not afford to buy any so I spent the last couple of months wearing my husband's tops and massive denim overalls…very becoming….NOT.

Our cat used to come walking with me, well by that stage waddling… and one day he chased a rabbit and was stuck in near a creek so I had to crawl through a fence to get him out…a sight in itself at 38 weeks pregnant, I had my stomach stuck in the fence on all fours… not the best outcome but made it back, a cross between the odd, well a few swear words, as I had crawled and basically rolled into the creek so was a moose covered in mud.

On one summer evening I was reading the birthing book, trust me, with your first child, this is not a good idea! I was 11 days overdue. This baby was not coming out but still kept growing!! 2kg a week…I had taken moose to a whole new level… not much weight on my body, just a huge baby jammed in a small body. I went to bed and felt strange so went to have a shower, about 10:30 at night….BANG! A sound from the baby..what on earth was that?? I called out to my Husband and said there is something wrong with the baby.. he came downstairs as I stood in water…oops! And then it began…labour…that is a whole different concept let me tell you…

So my caring (said with every ounce of sarcasm known to the planet..) husband, was busy checking if the dog was on heat while I dragged my suitcase into the car…sign?? And then left me at the door of the Maternity Hospital, outside, while he went to park the car, even though there were parks all empty right in front of him…

And a few hours later one of the most amazing things happened in my life. A huge baby boy was born, he was purple/ blue and breathing strangely so the Doctor took him away from me and they resuscitated him…I was taken to the shower. I was shaking in shock, I had a baby and they had taken him away. That part was not in the stupid birthing book. What did this mean? I was only 24. I did not understand why they took my baby. Apparently it was because they had given me pethidine too close to the birth so my baby came out basically stoned. I had to turn the water off as I felt too faint and sat in the shower alone crying. Finally, after just a few minutes, which, at the time felt like an eternity, I was wheeled up to see our son. He put his little head up from lying on his stomach and looked at me. And that was it…the most gratifying look from this little baby boy, well big baby boy, I was a Mother.

Naturally the family all came in with gifts and flowers and every aunty and every person's godmother, half of them I did not even know, all came in as I had produced the first grandson for the next generation… I felt like a broodmare…

So, all my friends were still going to the University Bar and there I was, sitting on a pad that resembled a surfing longboard in a bed in a Maternity Hospital with a baby boy who hated visitors and screamed every time somebody looked at him, except me. And we bonded. He hated the bath, I hated breast feeding. It was a fun time. He hated lying down so I sat him propped up and he was fine, only to be told by the nurses he should be lying down not half up so I ended up arguing with them which was great as they left me alone. After that they barely came in, I was obviously blacklisted… He would cry when ever they would change his nappy but was fine with me. I worked out he had to wear socks all the time. They used to change him with out socks and he would shake and scream, took me a day to work out, do not take his socks off!! To this day, that 28 year old boy always wears socks….how funny!

So wifey me brought the son and heir home from hospital…there was no wood in the shed…again…

It was summer so the top of the cottage was hot and the bottom was cold… Instead of rats there were spiders and a random snake on the verandah.

Cloth nappies adorned the clothesline and I would climb down the rock wall and hang them all out daily. Of course the dog had been on heat so when our baby was 10 weeks old we also had a pen on the verandah with 7 black puppies in it, who, once strong enough, would escape and run madly around the farm chasing cattle and sheep, with our black cat, who would bring home hares as big as himself and drop them on the kitchen floor in front of our baby in his rocker..

I felt like I was a nappy washer living in Noah's Ark.

Winter set in. Four month old baby in a freezing cold house. This was a new experience. The bedding would often be damp so I argued for a clothes dryer, the only godsend comfort I seemed to have. At times when I was freezing cold I felt like getting in the dryer myself. I spent the entire winter stoking the fire and keeping electric blankets going on beds to keep them dry.

You hear the stories of the World Wars and how women had to live while their husbands were away and this was nothing compared to what they all went through which gave me some kind of hope. In the meantime I joined a new Mother's session…Well that was like a competition for the grandest car, grandest designer dressed baby, they all had sealed nice houses with carpet and ovens that worked. I held a morning tea for them at the cottage once…oh dear…I could see the pity on their faces at the conditions for which we were living compared to them. And then when they left, our dog had brought a stiff possum as a present and delightfully placed it, with its legs in the air, on the front doormat…To this day, I do not believe they ever came back.

So it was our baby and I. My Husband still worked long hours, occasionally we would go for a walk but I felt like a single Mother right from the beginning. Was that a premonition? That winter seemed long as most winters on the island are. I spent it trying to keep the cottage warm, took a part time teaching job as we hardly had enough money for food. I took my baby boy to daycare…well…every week another ear infection, every day I would see that most of the babies were on antibiotics and then he would be sick again.

It was a fun time…. while I dreamed of a house with sealed walls and no possums looking at you through the roof at night ….and; actual heating! But, our baby boy was a joy and growing every day. It could have been alot worse! I was thankful for a bouncing baby and as time went on and summer came again, I tried the vegetable garden idea…again… This time whichever lettuces were not eaten by possums, cattle or sheep, were dug out by our son with his Tonka trucks…

I tried to make this marriage work…made cakes, made soup, made cushions, cleaned, designed..became the regular homemaker, basically lost all contact with my friends, who, of course, were all still partying at the University Bar. I had a few friends also on farms so occasionally there was some form of adult contact at a barbeque here and there.

So I fell pregnant again. Miscarried. Fell pregnant again. Miscarried. I was working as much as I could manage with a toddler. This, naturally did not suit my mother-in-law…she seemed to think that $28,000 a year income was going to be enough to live on forever and try to buy a house with a family… I fell pregnant again. There was no pressure to breed another boy as I had produced the son and heir to the throne. Obviously that meant that the family did not care about my trips in and out of hospital for three miscarriages. I came home one night a bit late as it was the Christmas Season so work was busy. I walked in the door and my mother-in-law grabbed me and started shaking me so hard that my necklace broke. Okay…this was different….

I was 25 or 26. Apparently I was not being the mother they expected because I had to have a job to basically keep the power on? Both my husband and mother-in-law spent about an hour yelling at me. I guess you could say that I had a fair go back at both of them and spent the night shut out of the bedroom sleeping in an armchair in my son's bedroom. Naturally I did not sleep, looked out over the river and at the moon shining over the paddocks towards the mountains.

That year I packed up our son and left my husband.

We moved to a dreadful Unit in a valley in the local city, in a valley in the local city meant it was literally freezing and did not get any sun at all. Another interesting time….as it was winter. The electric heater blew out some hot air but cost a fortune to run and there was no insulation so it basically did nothing. I was still young and not overly confident. The family came in and threatened to take the car (yes…from their grandson.. another sign that had a huge impact on the future fun times)

So I went back to my husband for the benefit of my son's welfare…. lasted three months on my own at 26 years old with a 2 year old.

We moved to the gatehouse of the massive calendar house where my husband's grandfather lived. It could not have been much worse…my mother-in-law would walk in at any given point, whether we were dressed or not. The aunties would turn up and occasionally random cousins when I would be bathing our son or trying to cook. I never really minded, only when dashing from the bathroom in a towel not realising they were all in the kitchen making coffee. Once again, it was not "my house"….infact, it felt less like my own space for our family than the cottage on the farm.

There were some positives, it had sealed walls and ceiling! That, in itself, was a brand new concept for me. It also had large windows that let the sun in, another new concept! The wood heater was quite exciting because it kept going!

But, there was a great big "but"…..

My mother-in-law….bless her…

I found it frustrating that she would keep trying to takeover my life, turn up at any given point, criticised anything that I made, criticised anything that I would plant, criticised if I worked, criticised if I did not work, basically criticised ME…

She gave us a red velvet lounge suite. Everything had to be red in her eyes in a house. To put things in perspective, she lived in a large house on their farm and all the way through the house was bright red carpet…. This lounge suite was dreadful. I tried to ease the pain with different cushions, but, it was just so RED!! Naturally I was stuck with the lounge suite. Everything in our home had to be exactly as my mother-in-law wished. There was no room for my creativity, it was just not accepted. I felt I had totally lost my identity!

So here I was, feeling like I was married to the family not my husband. Looking back now I really was just so young and naïve and had absolutely no idea what I was really doing apart from putting my heart and soul into creating a family. My parents were still on the Coast so I had no family support of my own apart from the endless hours on the phone to my mother.

Finally, after another visit from my mother-in-law in the bathroom while I was, once again, in the shower, I managed to find the courage to suggest to my husband that we move away in order to save our marriage! At first he was astonished, but he did start to see reason gradually over the next weeks. I explained that I felt smothered by the family, smothered by their expectations of me to constantly be babysitting my sister in law's child when she was 'tired'…. even though she was not working, had all the support of my mother-in-law and her mother-in-law, and I was juggling a toddler and work. I was expected to put our son in day care, yet on my days off, expected to babysit her daughter, which was another of my mother-in- law's ideas….The whole scenario was stifling to say the least.

Eventually, my husband decided we would move to the tropics! With my parents living on the Coast up there I saw hope, even though the position he took was in the city, an hour away, suddenly I had my family around my son and I. We lived in a leafy street in the suburbs and I was much more content raising our son, now age 3. Life for me revolved around my 3 year old as my husband's new position allowed for his hours to almost double. Therefore, we basically saw him one day a week. My son thought he was a robot?! He used to ask when that robot would visit and say hello….I think this was an indication of the time spent at work.

So I still felt completely alone with my son but once a week I was allowed to drive to see my family on the Coast. This was the best day of the week. To all couples out there, that was the key word….ALLOWED…I finally realised that I **had** completely lost my identity as well as the added bonus of living with my husband, a man I had grown to dream of playing pin the tail on the donkey on his face. I would clean the house, mow the lawns, take care of our son, do the gardening, washing, everything so that he could relax as he worked such long hours. This actually meant that he would sit on the couch drinking beer and watching television when home instead of thinking it might be nice to have a conversation with his wife, let alone go anywhere or do anything together as a family.

The one thing that I did realise was that I needed something to focus all my thoughts and energy on. My relationship was not good in any sense of the word. I wanted a baby girl with all of my heart. So, new focus, BABY GIRL….

Chapter 3

Baby girl....s

(deliberate misinterpretation of the English grammar)

So …baby girl…naturally I was terrified of the miscarriages that I had had and the effects on my body but figured that I might as well give it a go. I said to my mother that all I wanted was a baby girl with a bow in her hair…again. I would have been equally happy with a little boy to be my son's brother because I had the gut feeling that the first miscarriage was another boy.

It is a known fallacy that 'what you say is what you get' …well I wanted my baby girl to compliment having a gorgeous lively son. What I failed to ever really understand, but am totally in awe of, still…to this day…was having three baby girls in a row..yes…X3!! 3 born in 3 years. Well this was a clear indicator that our relationship was no longer either of our focus, my husband started working 13 days out of 14, an escape for him from his new family and I kept having babies so I could focus on that.

And, at the end of having four children under the age of seven, I was miraculously still slim and could wear jeans, possibly because every day was just so busy running around after a house full of little people!

Well, my advice to any of you girls out there, is if you really want to eventually test your already non-existent relationship, have four children in seven years…miraculous concept actually. My husband loved the children yes, in his funny way…'funny'…another interesting word in a relationship sense. It basically created a man who did not want to come home so he started working 13 – 15 hour days. Our son still thought he was a robot, the girls barely saw him as they would be asleep when he left for work and asleep when he returned. Some of the time I was so exhausted that I would be asleep too! There was hardly any family time as such. My husband was living his life and I was a single parent … with..a husband…

I devoted my days to my babies, dressed them in really cute clothes, created a wonderful garden while they played in the wading pool. In the summertime, living in the tropics, obviously it was hot so they were all little fish living in their little pool and late afternoon I used to take the shampoo out and wash their hair before emptying the pool for the day! My garden was my sanity and it grew and grew, and; before long, I had blocked out the neighbours and my babies and I lived in a beautiful oasis of shade!

Each birthday I would make a novelty cake that they would just love. Looking back on the many photos, there they all were, around a classic character cake, and there was that one glass of wine nearby…never two…my husband was never there for the birthdays generally. Maybe this was the premonition that I was going to be a single mother one day….famous last words! I already was.

So I had had two of my baby girls in the tropics and my husband had taken a position in the outback. I had been very pregnant with my fourth baby and we packed up the other three children, one budgie and one large dog and drove across Australia. That was an adventure at 28 weeks pregnant to say the least! We stopped at one point in the middle of nowhere and I got out and opened the back of the four wheel drive and our dog jumped out in excitement knocking the budgie cage down and the dogfood and myself. I picked myself up and got the dogfood out of my overalls… It was a terrific experience for our son and our toddler daughter. My baby daughter was just happily drinking her milk bottle looking out the window of the car.

Meeting the one and only Obstetrician in the town was fascinating…first thing he told me was that he used to be a Vet….and preceded to explain that delivering a child is basically the same as delivering a foal. I just looked at him and thanked him very much for his time…..and had my baby girl in the city instead.

The outback was a distraction from my dull marriage. I made friends with some girls who had children of the same ages and the days passed happily with children swimming and playing while we consumed copious amounts of champagne.

Chapter 4

Almost losing a child

I do not believe there is any challenge greater than a sick child. And, I know there is no greater challenge than having a medical emergency with a child where you are told they may only have 4 hours to live. Life was busy with 3 babies and getting my son to school in amongst nappies, feeding, locating the crawler and generally trying not to lose one somewhere. 4 under 7 is a lot of handling, at times I felt like a gymnast.

My son was a busy little boy and doing taekwondo, his newest love. He managed to get a cold at school and as we all know, that is so common in children. This one was different. Children normally shake a cold or flu type illness but he did not seem to be bouncing back very quickly. We were on about day 3 so I took him to the local doctor. Usual story, give him Panadol, fluids and rest as it is a virus. Another 2 days went by, no improvement, infact he was more tired it appeared and spent the day on the couch watching television. I took him back to the doctor. Panadol, fluids and rest was the diagnosis..again. I am not sure this doctor realised how much effort it was to pack up 3 babies into the car, bottles, food, nappies, double pram for a 30 second visit with the same diagnosis. I was starting to feel frustrated. The next morning my son did not get out of bed. I was beginning to worry. This was starting to appear a bit unusual.

He finally got up and told me that his legs were sore. He was limping but it was more like rocking from one leg to the other. He reached out to his glass of water and knocked it off the bedside table. I asked if he was okay and he said his hands felt funny. I called the doctor and off we went again. The doctor said he must have a taekwondo injury hence his legs not working well. I did question this only to be told that he was the doctor and I did not know what I was talking about. I was so angry leaving the surgery. I took all 4 of them home… again. I called

15

my husband's boss as his wife was a registered nurse and asked if she would come and have a look at my son.

At the time I was ironing and let her speak to my son without me. She came back into the kitchen and said he had no facial muscles working and that he was complaining about pain in his neck. She was white as a ghost. I just looked at her and turned the iron off. She offered to babysit the girls as I packed my son into the car, now barely walking. He was becoming breathless. I felt like I was playing part in the worst horror drama any parent could manage as we drove straight to the Emergency Department at the local hospital. I parked at the door and my son said he could not stand. There was a lady nearby that I called out to and she helped me carry him straight in. My son asked what was happening. I managed to smile at him and held his little 7 year old hand saying for him not to worry, to look at mummy's eyes and that everything was going to be okay.

He was promptly examined by the Paediatrician who pulled me aside and said it looks to be Guillian Barre Syndrome, an allergic reaction to the virus he had had. They explained that they had no ventilators in the outback so we would need to be airlifted to Children's Hospital in the city. Suddenly nothing in the world mattered. The hospital had contacted my husband and he was on his way. They told me to race home and pack clothes for myself, I remember asking how long would we would be in the city and they said hurry because he has about 4 hours to live if we do not get him there. They told me to pack enough for anywhere between 6 months to 3 years…As I rushed off I asked why so long and they just said because he will have to learn to walk again. I drove the car home. I could not even drive fast. I was like a snail driving with tears streaming down my face, my hands shaking on the gearstick.

I threw goodness knows what in a bag and headed back. My husband was now home so I knew the girls would be okay. By the time I got back to the hospital the ambulance was there and my son was on a stretcher plugged into every type of ECG wire anything and on oxygen and being loaded into the ambulance, I jumped in and before we knew it we were on a Royal Flying Doctor flight headed for the city.

It was dark flying and the staff were all very calm. I did hear the Captain on the radio telling somebody they could not pick up a child with a burn on the way because they were carrying a child about to die…I do not think that I was supposed to hear that. That 1.5 hours holding his little hand and trying so hard to smile at him and not dissolve into a mass of tears was one of the most difficult things that I have done.

When we landed in the city there was an ambulance on the tarmac, lights flashing. We were taken straight to the children's hospital in the city, straight in the doors so fast I was basically running alongside the stretcher. My son's body was losing control and he was thrashing around in pain and vomiting. I was taken out shaking as a nurse held me uncontrollably crying. This was the worst moment of my life. They calmed me down and said that I would see him in a few minutes and he would be calm, that he was in the best place.

I was soon allowed in and my son was calm, lying flat on oxygen. He had no strength and could not even lift his hand to hold mine. I just held his hand gently as they said that his nervous system was shutting down so touching him will hurt. I remember thinking anything else?? Now the nervous system? 6 hours previously I had just been ironing and planning what to cook for dinner…

So I learnt a lot in my time in the children's hospital. Guillian Barre starts in the hands and the feet and basically works its way to the lungs, hence the panic as my son had it in his lungs by the time we got to the hospital. I was told it was an allergic reaction to the virus that my son had had whereby the red blood cells and white blood cells fight each other and not the virus causing the nervous system to begin shutting down.

We were placed in quarantine the first few days and I could stay at the hospital as I was an outback parent. The Neurologist and the entire team were nothing short of amazing. I had been sitting at his bedside for what seemed like days and the staff took me aside and said my lips had gone blue and I was dehydrated so they filled me up with water and sandwiches. I remember asking if my son was going to live. That was a good day. They said yes! They explained that he was responding to the instagam blood plasma drip that he was on for the first 5 days really well.

The next morning I got up in my little room as they started making me get some sleep so I could function and walked down the hallway. I saw my son raise his little hand and wave. I just cried. He had the biggest and strongest grin on his little face! He could move his limbs again.

So we became part of the hospital life, it became home for the short time we were there. I used to have to help bath my son on a stretcher over a big bath and, of course made it fun by hosing him in the face and making him laugh again once he was a little stronger. He could not walk, he spent each day lying flat. I got some texta pens once he could move his hands again and we spent our days drawing Sesame Street characters and giving pictures to the other sick children in the ward. There was a little baby next to us who did not look right one morning and was taken away swiftly and never brought back. That was a bit of a reality check. There was a delightful little girl who had lived there 6 months and had fallen through scaffolding on her parent's home they were building, 3 floors high. She had some sort of head injury and spinal defects but was chatty in her own little way and always smiling. The attitude of sick children is something all adults should embrace because they still smile and are happy!

My son started to walk again and sit up in his bed. His determination and also fitness even at that age had been good to him. I encouraged him every day and we set little goals like walk to that chair over there, each day making the distance longer.

Finally he was discharged. I kept him home from school for a while, a couple of weeks if not longer from memory and had to try explaining to the little ones to not climb all over their brother until he was stronger. From there we changed doctors in the outback. I remember seeing him one day and he apologised. I just looked at him and said it was not his fault. What went through my mind was not what I said, but I thought well what advantage would that be? Everyone makes a mistake at some point, his time was now, but that was not for me to say.

Chapter 5

3 states in 1 year

Naturally after having been pregnant for three years, and my son almost not making it, my mother and father came to stay. She had not been well but she and my father flew to visit. My mother happened to say in lighthearted conversation, so are you having another baby next year or are you actually going to address the fact that you should think about divorce? My mother …possibly the reason why I am so blunt myself, she never held back with her thoughts. It did plant a seed in my mind though, even though being in the middle of the outback of Australia, was not really an ideal place to be thinking of how to end my marriage and potentially pack up four young children, a dog and a budgie and start driving home to the tropics. It was a bit far….

So, I waited, naturally my husband claimed he resigned, I found out later he was actually fired…. And I had to pack up an entire house in three days with all the children as they had only given him a week's notice and the house was part of the package we were on….awesome… easy job with a 15 month old, who, thankfully, was too chubby to yet walk and a 2 month old baby. My 3 year old baby girl became a huge help entertaining my baby and 'locating' her sister crawling all over the house getting lost in packing paper. She also helped feed them both. I was on a stressful time frame to be packed. I remember walking past the high chair with more boxes watching my eldest daughter with her head in the fridge and asked her to close the door then noticed my middle daughter in the high chair chewing on raw pumpkin… I explained to my 3 year old that the babies cannot have raw pumpkin to which she asked if baby wanted a coffee…no darling….

How is it that some girls seem to meet Mr Right or their 'Man from Snowy River' and flow into the perfect marriage with the picket fence and never have a care in the world while their husband takes care of everything? And then there is US…as I presume you, who are reading this and laughing with your glass of wine in hand, only having picked this book up to appreciate how eventful my life has been, perhaps realise your life is actually not too bad, or, all of the above…

But that is the point, I am not here to complain about the hard cards I have been dealt, I am here to share that every step I am deeply thankful for, just as you can be if you so choose! I am a firm believer in fate and destiny and that there is a reason for everything that crosses your path and the decisions made. The reasons take you to your next adventure, your next destination in your adventure. Life is an adventure and that bad 'stuff' is just stuff testing your strength and endurance.

So we drove home to the tropics. 31 years old now, mother of 4.

4 young children, 1 dog and 1 budgie, even the dog looked at me as we put him in the car, it was a look of Are you actually kidding me… off we travelled again. My husband thought it a good idea to leave the outback at 2pm….so naturally we arrived at the beginning of the plains too late to get accommodation and had to keep driving overnight. I swear I have never seen so much wildlife but the babies all slept thankfully and we arrived across safely and totally exhausted after sharing a 25 hour straight journey overnight, dodging tall red kangaroos that could potentially have sent the car radiator into the front seats had we hit them. Thankfully, we did not, for our sake and theirs. A note to anybody likely to venture across our great sunburnt plains of the outback of Australia, DO NOT DRIVE OVERNIGHT. It is just too risky, particularly if you have not lived on farms and understand watching fencelines and movement.

This was the start of a spectacular year! Of course a hint of extreme sarcasm of the word. Obviously, me saying that does entail I was driving into the Eastern sun that morning not yet realising the extent of what I was facing. I think this really was the beginning of a journey for which I was clearly not prepared.

My mother became extremely ill when we arrived back in the tropics and as well as settling back into to our little home I was faced with a very difficult 5 months until my mother's passing, but a lot of very special memories with my children and their beloved Nanny.

My husband decided we were to go back to the island so he could take over the family timber operations, said to me while I was in the process of facing losing my mother… I remember just looking at him in disbelief, trying to warm to the idea but thinking that the timing could not have ever been worse. Back to my mother-in-law…….So I was running open homes at our house in the tropics to sell it, a house with white tiles in the kitchen and four small children…disaster!!

Within this year, the babies all grew and we had happy times every day. These 4 little people that I was lucky enough to be their mother, were my life, my entirety, Katerina was no longer a person, I spent my days singing children's songs while scrubbing the shower. And; do you know, the days as their mother are the happiest days anyone could ever hope for. So there were, of course, all the regular moments as a parent…

There were the goldfish, that episode did not end well. I never seemed to grasp the correct format to being a fish parent…my son once saying, on about fish pet number 6, "Mum, why is Max swimming in the toilet?"

There was the bath time looking for which little person had done their toilet training situation in front of Bananas in Pyjamas children's program in amongst the Duplo and toys on the carpet. Yes, located.

Then there was the wading pool under our outdoor shade cover as the Brisbane summers were hot. I discovered the best way to bath all 4 children at once: hint to all parents..take the soap and shampoo outside to the pool instead of the other way around! The only problem with that, of course, was that the dog decided at times to join in so there were a couple of grey areas as to who went first and who tried to help me by shampooing their hair with the dog shampoo. Needless to say, the children never had fleas either..

Then my first daughter decided she was ready for toilet training, this was quite easy for my son as I used to put Christmas balls from the tree in the toilet for him to aim for, worked well until after a couple of times the decorations would flush and I eventually blocked the entire system and had to try to explain to a Plumber as to why there were Christmas decorations blocking the plumbing. This time was different and my daughter was very keen to wear panties so it was relatively easy. However, during that time she used to flush the whole toilet roll every visit to the bathroom and with the 2 younger babies, it was virtually impossible to be everywhere for all of them all the time, this, of course ended up with the girls in the local supermarket looking at me in a weird manner as I used to have to buy toilet rolls by the dozen…daily.

Obviously being a hot climate, the toys dissipated to outside as well, the Sesame Street rubber figurines finally found days later having been chewed by the dog.

In amongst the trips taking the children down to see my ailing Mother, the open homes where I had to turn a house designed for a family with maximum 1 child, not 4, into a complete display home twice a week so people would buy it leaving me with the excitement (not) of moving back to the farm my mother in law was at. Soon after my Mother passed, the house sold. At this point, the children were the only excitement in my life, being there to support my Father grieve and packing up a house with 4 small children.

And there it was….the year 2000, we moved from the outback to the tropics, lost my mother and then we moved from the tropics to the island…with 4 small children, a dog and a budgie… and; once again, we drove…Three states resided in within a 12 month period. Who does that? Any marriage that can handle that must mean that you have found the illusive "one". At this point, I can honestly say I felt not any feeling or form of emotion for my husband. I used to look at him snoring on the couch wondering how on earth I was supposed to live with him forever. I am quite sure he felt the same way about me yelling at him in frustration.

Landing at the farm: here we were, unpacking to stay at my father and mother in law's house, planning to build our own house, on their farm, in the next paddock, approximately 300m from their house. It was decided we were to rent a cottage in the nearby village while we built the house that only my husband, father and mother in Law seemed to be allowed to agree over. I did not seem to be asked for an opinion. I found humour in this whole situation by walking at night across the paddocks looking at the site for the house, laughing to myself that my husband was now at home with his parents and would bath the children with her at night like I no longer existed. But, after all the years I had done it, I actually used to walk over to a rock in the far paddock and dream and wonder where on earth I belonged and then come back to tuck my babies into bed. It was about time he actually learnt about bathing 4 children in any case for I had done it alone for years.

I remember one night that I just sat there on that rock in the paddock thinking to myself: is this it? Is this my life? Is this smothered situation all I was to live with this family controlling all that I did and, not only that…was! I thought to myself, is a great big car going to take me away from here one day in a box, after making my 600th pot of pumpkin soup wearing an apron after spending my life watching my husband sit there watching television and not talk to me?

I stood up, age 32 and that was it…in the back of my mind I knew. I wanted Katerina back, I had gone! I had no idea how or when my return would happen, my priority was my children, but somehow, in amongst being a mother, I knew I had to incorporate me! I guess it was my "Bridget Jone's Diary"[2] moment.

Have any of you ever felt completely lost? Like you have become so involved in a situation that has just unfolded without much thought or choice, but more through circumstance? At 32, this was my life. I could not even call my mother anymore. I called my father daily and he was always a great support but different conversation than my mother. It was a very trying few months over the summer.

---

[2] *Bridget Jone's Diary,* Universal Pictures, Little Bird, Studio Canal, Working Title Films, (2001).

Chapter 6

The Mouse House

Right before Christmas that year, we moved into the only rental property available in the village. Here I introduce The Mouse House, a house from a time where it was acceptable to live in an uninhabitable residence. There were 2 bedrooms and a small sunroom out off the kitchen. The bathroom had a ceiling covered in mould. There was a huge grassed yard, I do not think it worthy of being called a garden, it was surrounded by hedges which the children played in on their cute adventures when my son made the girls actually believe they were Power Rangers.

The sunroom was also damp and mouldy so I made sure the children were all sleeping in the main part of the house so they would not become ill. My husband became busy over on the farm with his parents developing the timber business, I became the stay at home mother so, once again, it was the children and I, which, I have to say was when I was at my happiest. We developed our routines and my husband really did not have much to do with us, even with his new found freedom of managing his own hours of work and enjoying his evenings drinking gins with his parents on their verandah.

I think this particular summer, I spent hours sitting out in the large yard dreaming of one day having pot plants again like I had had in our little home in the tropics. I would smile watching the children all outside playing, sipping on my wine just thinking. I had watched my Parents over the 35 year wonderful marriage that they had lived before my Mother was taken from us.

I think when you get married you do believe you are embarking on a fairytale, although, for me, I never actually had those thoughts. It was almost expected as our families were all so closely entwined socially that if I had not married my Husband, it would have been strange at the time. My parents were a fairytale couple. You could see the chemistry, the friendship underlying and the love they had for each other every day. What I was in…was not like that!

The subject of arranged marriages comes to mind as I write this. We were a couple who were driven together and everybody was so happy we had married…except us. I do not believe my husband was happy either. If he had been, he might have actually spent some time with the children and I, but, as the summer went on, he just spent more time over with his parents. It was apparent that the children and myself were just an accessory when they invited guests and relatives over for barbeques. Noting that, once again, I say 'they'.….as in I was married to the family, not him.

Never, in a million years did I foresee the following events that transpired. I believe I knew that he and I would not be together forever, I certainly did not envisage the way it all happened.

You may be thinking why was this little mould ridden cottage named The Mouse House. Interestingly my son was growing into a really mature little boy and he followed me to the linen cupboard, which was right next to the back door, which, I used to have to leave open even if It was cold because it was the only way the children could access the yard, yet the doorhandle was at adult level in height. The mice had relocated to the linen cupboard and had progressively eaten through all my late mother's beautiful linen, they ate through sheets and underneath the frequently used towels and sheets was a complete disaster zone where everything so special had holes in it. I was devastated at the time. I think this was the point where I started thinking what was the next disaster coming for me?

Little did I know…

Chapter 7

The Oven

Still, to this day, I have friends and acquaintances that comment to me on parts of this chapter in sheer disbelief as to how I managed to survive and raise the beautiful adult 4 of today.

Have any of you ever had a marriage actually end over an oven? Oh yes, well let me enlighten you on this gallant experience. We are infact talking here about an oven that was to be ordered for our house by my parents-in-law and my husband, a house that had not been built yet…

It was just a regular afternoon in the Mouse House with dinner cooking and me running around getting pyjamas ready for the 4 children in the bath, 2 of which were still in nappies. I called my husband and asked if he was able to bring more milk home. He said he was sitting on his parent's verandah drinking Gins with the 'oven man' deciding on an oven for our house, that was still just a paddock.

I have to say, the feisty side of my personality showed itself, what the actual…??? I said to him ever so sarcastically, why were they choosing an oven for a paddock, were we to put an oven in the grass and build the house around the oven? And, why was I not part of the conversation considering that I would be the person who was to be cooking in said oven? Obviously, my husband became irate at my 'apparent' lack of respect for his parents (?) and said that he was leaving me. This came as a massive shock as I sipped my wine and noticed the children had all got out of the bath themselves and were currently laughing their little hearts out running around the yard naked.

So I forced every ounce of courageous anger and told my husband FINE….and we all know that if a girl says fine, generally it does mean that it is far from fine. I asked if he could please get the milk on his way over to pack his bags.

I managed to get the children into their pyjamas whilst running through the yard on this tranquil summer's night, looking at their eyes knowing that their father was about to come through the door, pack his bag and leave us forever. Ironically, I did not feel sad, or even angry actually. I think using the word before, tranquil, really summed up that night. It was over. This twisted, toxic marriage was about to end forever. That part I knew. This time there was not going to be any going back. I guess, in a way, it just made it easier that he left us and not the other way around.

So, 30 minutes later on April 20, 2001, my husband came home to the glorious Mouse House with a bunch of roses and the milk. I gave the roses back to him and told him to give them to his mother. I took the milk, possibly the last thing that man ever gave me apart from Divorce Papers. I also told him a few other things that he could tell his mother, which, are not really appropriate to spell out so shall remain a little mystery, however, I do feel if any of you have had a man put you in 2 houses full of mice, left you at a hospital entrance where you fainted having a miscarriage and then was packing a bag leaving you with 4 small children to go and live with his mother, I am pretty sure you can figure out a few choice words.

The little girls were all playing and basically oblivious to the fact that their father was leaving. My son, however, was right onto it. He stood beside me and watched his father leave. I closed the door. My son said, "Oh well, that's the end of him". I have to say that did surprise me, but then, all the years of this man not spending much time with the children, which, was his choice, not mine, it suddenly did not surprise me.

Chapter 8

Welcome to single parenthood

I t was a sunny day when I woke up as a single parent. Routine was no different to any other day getting the children ready for school. My son was in year 3 at the nearby farm school approximately 10 kilometres further toward the mountains. My first daughter had just started kindergarten wearing a school dress that was so long as she was not tall. I bought her a bucket hat but she cried as she wanted a legionaires hat, which, covered most of her face and she kept running into things, but she was very happy. The babies would come in the car to school with me to drop the 2 bigger ones off. This day was no different, apart from my second daughter singing "Daddy's gone" all the way in the car to school and then my littlest, and third daughter, of course tried her utmost to copy her sister which was a little embarrassing as it continued into the kindergarten classroom.

I drove the little babies back home and then started to think what on earth I was to do. We needed groceries and any form of normality was a treat today as it merely removed my thoughts from the fact that my husband had gone. He did not call all day to see how we were, this was quite typical of him so not actually any different to the last 10 years of marriage really.

We drove to the nearby town for groceries, which was always an experience with a baby in nappies and the other thinking she was toilet trained but actually was not quite there, which, became apparent when I sat her on a seat then picked her up to see the large wet patch. So I filled up the trolley with groceries, my thoughts were, that I could start to digest what had actually happened back home knowing that I had a week's food for the children. The worst maternal nightmare happened at the checkout….that one thing everyone dreads, particularly with two little children in the trolley who were now tired, irritable and starting to pinch each other making the other cry, yes, well timed that we were finished shopping!

The debit card declined. I knew that there was money to buy food in that joint account, otherwise I would not have spent 30 minutes filling the trolley! It declined again. I felt my cheeks start to burn in embarrassment as I released both my little ones from the trolley and we left the supermarket without any food. We arrived back home in the village, 20 minutes out of the main town. I called the bank. They explained that my now ex husband had been in and taken all of the money from our account leaving me with a glorious balance of $3.52. I tried to call my ex husband and he did not answer the phone, literally all day.

And there I was, a girl left in a house full of mould and mice, 4 small children, 1 dog, 1 budgie, no husband and $3.52 to my name. Well, I decided there was no point crying after figuring out my situation. That was not going to solve the pantry problem.

I packed the little ones into the car for a journey to the other side of the main town to the Government Department. I had to apply for benefits. In Australia we are very lucky that our Government does provide this as an option for "people like myself" who, as they strategically explained it to me, were "left for dead". This was not a proud moment…Naturally, my second daughter told them "Daddy's gone" as well. I felt tears welling up in my eyes, this was my emotional moment, I guess it had to happen at some point.

This was Friday so the money available to me would be in my new bank account I had to open until Monday, therefore, we were basically running out of food over the weekend, that was something to look forward to I thought, shrugging my shoulders at the girl who clearly was looking at me like she hoped that would never happen to her. I also was hoping that it would not happen to her. It should not happen in this deliberate and nasty manner to any human being, particularly their own children.

This was only the beginning….

Had I known the transformation of my life in the next few weeks, I would have been somewhat prepared, however, I do not think in a cruel way so I had no idea of the events that were all about to take place.

Friday afternoon. I packed up the little ones into the car and drove out the straight farm road towards the mountains and the lovely little school the children were attending. I walked into the kindergarten and the Teacher's Aide, whom I am still in touch with all these years later, put her hand on my arm and asked if I was okay. Apart from my father and my brother, she was the first person that knew. She told me that my first daughter had gallantly shared our very personal news for show and tell. Of course, being a small country town surrounded by farms, and quite a number of the mothers being involved with the school day, the entire district knew by this afternoon that I was suddenly a single parent in a very small and gossiping village, with 4 small children. Great.

Later that night after I had the children all fed, bathed and asleep, my ex husband decided to visit, unannounced. Fortunately, before his entry, I had managed to squeeze the last half glass of wine from the cask. And, did I need that after this chain of events. I noticed his father out in their SAAB motor vehicle (no expense spared when it came to their vehicles…) with the engine running. I was a bit confused at this point. My ex husband grabbed my wallet from the drawer, I asked what he was doing, to which he replied, taking all that is mine. I said to him that he had left me with no money for food for the children and to this day, I will never forget his response. Apparently it was not his problem anymore. He then went on to say that he wanted to destroy me and watch me grovel in a gutter. I said, in amongst a few choice words we both shared, that he could take the shirt from my back but, so help me God, he would never destroy me.

Silly me, I did not think to take the $5,000 credit card and make that money disappear. Silly me for being an honest and nice person in this situation! I sat and thought a lot that night, firstly, glad, after his behaviour and clear lack of responsibility for 4 children, that I was glad this had happened now and I did not waste any further years of my life on cooking for this man.

There were suddenly so many wonderfully positive thoughts. I think, my point being, and now looking back, people's relationships sometimes do not work, no matter how hard they try, no matter what they do, how they mediate, some things are just plainly NOT MEANT TO BE, and that marriage had a great big red flashing light on it, that it had not, and was never, going to work.

My late mother always bought my ex husband jars of mustard for every Christmas, I never really understood why until in her final days she told me she never liked him and hoped it would upset his stomach. Okay Mum, that was a dark thought! At this point of my Friday, I could have ordered him a 44 gallon drum of mustard, but, instead, I was just thankful for the extra 3 litres of milk he had given me before he left me with 4 children and $3.52.

The weekend was relaxed, the children all playing outside and having fun. It is quite surprising when you do not have any money, how little you need it. We stayed home that weekend, conserving fuel mostly and I found ways of making shortbread and cake for school lunches and utilising the neighbour's plum tree that hung over the fence for extra fruit. Of course the gossip had begun, being such a small town and many people who I really did not know suddenly were all walking their dogs past our house, driving past, ironically, not one of them calling in to see if I needed any help. All typically amusing really.

Life started to just move along relatively normally for a few weeks, my ex husband did not ask to, nor spoke with, the children for 6 weeks. Life became quite peaceful and I just got on with it really. I used to sit on a stool near the kitchen window and stare out at the plantless yard at night with a candle burning, enjoying a wine after the children were in bed. I had no direction, was losing weight by day, but I was just in survival mode for the time being.

Chapter 9

And then everything else went!

Our new semi normal life was coasting along....until...

My ex husband and brother in law wanted to come and collect his personal belongings ie, 21st presents, a table, few painting etc so I did the right thing and left the house so they could come and go without the children and I home.

During this strange set of circumstances, I am not sure where the boundaries for theft were set, but he certainly had no boundaries.

We arrived home 2 hours later. They had left the doors and windows open, it was freezing cold and the woodheater was out. It was nothing short of a deliberate act of horrid behaviour towards me. We walked inside and he had taken the children's beds. He had taken their wardrobes. He had taken the table and chairs, the pots, the knives, the lamps, and his own personal effects, which, I had said was fine. Glasses, cutlery, all sorts of items were gone. They had left the children's clothes on the floor. I frowned in complete disbelief. How can a human being do this to their own children? Who honestly cared if he had woken up one day and decided he hated his wife for whatever reason, that I really still do not know, but to take from his own children?

My son was a little champion and ran around collecting kindling to get the woodfire going again and that night for dinner I said to the children that we were having a Japanese dinner sitting on cushions on a picnic rug, because there was no table! I made the most out of what was becoming a really difficult situation! I made every day fun in our home. I also contacted a great old friend who was a Lawyer, as, if this was where my ex husband was heading playing these games, it was only a matter of time and he would commence parenting action. Finally,

I was starting to live my life like a game of monopoly, only difference being, that I was not landing on the lucky squares.

The following week, my ex husband had our motor vehicle collected by very serious looking men wearing suits. Great. I removed the car seats and watched our motor vehicle being driven away. Right, well this has to be all, I remember actually laughing to myself, there is nothing more he can strip from us? Surely…I poured myself a calming glass of wine. I told myself, I can do this. I can do this, holding back tears of desperation, looking at my laughing, healthy, happy children who knew that I would hold it together, yes, I can do this, well I had to do this, there was not another option!

So there I was, it was winter in the village, we had mattresses on the floor to sleep on, 1 pot I managed to buy on sale, 1 knife and no means of transport. I really could not understand, and still, to this day, do not understand how he felt it okay to hurt his own children. It is one topic, for a relationship to breakdown, but the children should still be looked after. Light shone on that subject when I considered my other sister in laws, whereby my ex mother in law made sure that everything those girls had was also taken, and they had children too. So my ex mother in law made it her whole focus to take everything she could from us and, my ex husband just followed every idea she came up with.

So, I did not dwell on any of this, I worked on gaining a little support group of other parents from the school and gradually built age old friendships with friends that I had grown up with. My father and brother organised a little 2 door cheap motor vehicle that I could run the children out to school in and life went on. My father was a great support and, apart from being on the coast, I still had phone conversations daily, both holding our glass of wine and laughing at this year so far. I had decided there was nothing else to do but laugh, no point being down about it, I had 4 healthy gorgeous little children and they gave me such joy.

Approximately 6 weeks into my newly single life as a mother, of course the topic of vulnerability reared its head, something that I can see so clearly in others now looking back, however, could not read myself back then.

Chapter 10

The School Teacher

Enter the charming School Teacher….

Naturally, I fell automatically into his strong arms, gazing into his baby blue eyes… the stupidity of falling so easily not even contemplated by myself. I was infatuated. It all started with utmost attention at any school events, a load of wood delivered to help out the new single mother, I should have seen this one coming but NO….I went to mush and for a brief delirious moment thought I had fallen in love… Needless to say he convinced me that he was divorced, which I believed, until I discovered his wife driving past my house about 4-5 times a day and then questioned him. Silly me. Fell into that trap! Silly Katerina had even written a stupid romantic poem to this man who I did not know was still married?! Yes… just when you think you are growing up…

Ironically, his wife managed to locate and meet my ex husband. The School Teacher went to their house one evening after I had ended our short fling finding out about his wife, another girlfriend and that they were having problems...to find my ex husband hiding in their bedroom wardrobe. Oh the webs people spin….

This, I found, hilarious.

By this stage, the children had started going to the farm for weekend time with their father and grandparents and about 2 weeks after the wardrobe incident, the School Teacher's wife was also staying at the grandparent's house with my children. Because of the nature of the speed of their relationship, they then created a fabulous tale that I had been having an affair with the School Teacher since the year before, which, did not work as we had been living in the tropics and I had not met him. So, in amongst my children getting used to going to their father's farm, they suddenly had a new step mother painting the inside of the new house that we were meant to be building together, that they had only met the first weekend she stayed out there. I was instructed by my Lawyer to just always make my home a happy place, I focussed on those words for their entire childhood and those words would be my advice to you, especially when the third party appears out of nowhere or a wardrobe carrying a paintbrush…

Suddenly I heard about this wonderful new home being built, while we were still living in the Mouse House, attending the children's sporting events watching her pretending to play happy families hanging onto my ex husband for dear life. In any case, he backed off being so mean to me as he was too busy keeping her happy and building the house. Things were good. At this point I realised how peaceful it was to be single. I soon became used to all of the village gossip. Because my ex husband had moved his new partner to the farm so quickly, infact, while I was actually never sure if she was even separated from the charming School Teacher, they decided to gloat on the 'I had the affair' story to justify themselves. I really could not have cared less!

I think him moving on so quickly and seriously it seemed, broke me for a little bit. Do not misinterpret that comment. I did not want him back. I think at the time I felt like I had given up my whole life and career to be the homemaker and had moved the children all over the country for his career to be left in a house full of mice with all the children and nothing. My ex husband had certainly moved on with his new lady to forget the timeline of when we had actually moved our 4 children to the farm. Had he completely forgotten that he had moved us here to suit his own career move, for a few months, and then abandoned us? I suddenly felt exactly that, abandoned. I was the first to admit, in relationship terms we had never worked out, but for him to not even be able to work out when he had uprooted his young family and then left us in a mould ridden house full of mice, was absolutely beyond me. But here he was painting the house with another woman literally 3 months after he had left us. I was glad that it was not me designing that as my destiny, but to anyone who splits up, please consider some time alone with the children by yourself before jumping into living with a new partner.

Chapter 11

The hardest yards

So, I just got on with life really. I did not miss the farm. I certainly did not miss watching him drinking beer and watching Baywatch drooling over Pamela Anderson. I felt like every bored village person was watching my every move for some new gossip on the single mother of 4. I heard in the local shop one day, some people talking about 'the blonde in the silver car' and then I pushed my trolley into their aisle and they all went silent….oh that was obviously me… Excellent, I was now a celebrity.

The charming School Teacher was long gone, there were no more loads of wood delivered. It was just the children and I. It is strange how people in a small village can talk about you because you are raising 4 children alone living in a house not fit for human life, with a surname of a wealthy family who all drove nice cars and had $40,000 paintings hanging in their homes, yet none of them put their hand up to help out their own children/grandchildren/nieces/nephew. I think this was the point I lost most of my usual confidence.

I put my heart and soul into my children, drove them all to taekwondo, took goldfish in Tupperware containers for show and tell at school, yes, that one ended up dying too! I buried my head in keeping the bathroom coated in exit mould, splitting wood to keep the house dry, warm was just a dream, dry was paramount so the children would not become sick. My life was washing, cooking, driving, cleaning up after a dog, budgie and now rabbit, mowing lawns with a lawnmower that was just a great big cloud of smoke going up and down the grass, it was not lawn, just weeds mown flat really, and trying to keep them fed and clothed to the best to my ability. I felt dreadful that they only had mattresses and not beds but I just had no excess money to buy beds! On the upside they used to laugh and wrestle on the mattresses and practice their taekwondo moves so my house became a martial arts studio. I managed to get some cheap second hand bikes that were left at the tip, it was always touch and go when the children would take off on them as to whether or not the wheels would stay on and we would wind up in the emergency department. But they were happy, we had nothing, but it showed me that I could do it alone, we had a fridge full of food and a great big fruit bowl, and 4 happy little children.

Naturally I was a bit of a mess, I had lost about 10kgs in weight focussing on my children and not myself. I think this is a natural progression based on stress. My ex husband had built the house on the farm and my children were all given paint colours to choose for their bedrooms. Their now step mother was in glee at every sporting or school event smiling at me in the most sarcastic manner hanging onto my ex husband. He had even bought a car exactly the same model as the one he had taken from me, that she would be seen driving in. It was all supposed to upset me. It did not upset me as in ME. It upset me in terms of the children and that suddenly her children were all also enrolled in taekwondo and my ex husband would be taking them to training instead of taking mine.

Then, it happened. I was served with the Application for Divorce Papers. Oh good, I thought, it cost $250 to file in the Family Court and I no longer wanted to be married but that was a whole week's grocery money so never went down that track. Bingo, he was engaged.

Taekwondo training one cold Wednesday night I packed the children up to head home in the fog and was chased out the door by my ex husband's new fiancé who started screaming at me down the street. I remember turning, my 2 youngest daughters hanging onto me, one I was carrying and the other hanging onto my leg. She was screaming that she did not want to have my children for the weekend because they had a function to attend. My ex husband chased her down the street asking her to stop screaming at me. Surprisingly, when somebody makes me really angry my feisty nature subsides and I become eerily quiet, oh yes, so proud I was disciplining myself into keeping my 'cool'. I think this is seriously a gift I have developed after so much has gone wrong!!

She screamed at me that 'this'…was all my fault. I smiled, putting the little ones in my car and asked her what her interpretation of 'this' was…. I have to say I was very confused as to why she was so angry.

"Oh?" I said, "your engagement, is all my fault?"

"You stole my husband!" she replied angrily.

And there it was. I was back!! Katerina was back!! A strong, independent, still ever so slightly messed up, but getting there, Katerina, was back. I felt confidence inside myself for the first time in ages as I tried wholeheartedly not to laugh.

My ex husband was standing behind her as she wailed uncontrollably calling me all the names she could muster, infact, it was like an outback muster of names that went on for days droving the cattle to home. I just stood there.

"Are you finished?" I interrupted eventually.

She kept on going. I held my hand up like a stop sign.

"Firstly, you can have your husband back because I had no idea he was married at the time and do not see him now, months later. Secondly, congratulations on your engagement, (I looked past her to my ex husband) I thought you should really be a bit happier being engaged". I smiled at them both, got in the car and left.

I do believe, being a woman of any of our kind, that at any given point of your life to be a little thinner than someone who has decided you are their apparent rival, is a confidence building moment…even if it was thinner because of sheer stress of a pending Divorce, starving yourself while cooking for your children, forgetting to eat and waking up on the floor with a broken wineglass next to the woodfire and your bank statement, in the middle of the night while your babies slept peacefully, blowing out the candle that could have easily burnt the house down had you not frozen enough to wake up to go to bed, in your mould ridden house that, also, had no fitted smoke alarms, just one that used to sit on the bookcase and go off when I used the unsafe grill so I threw it into a pot plant outside the door. The bookcase…I had not thought we could have actually used that face down as a table either?!

Every day I would talk on the phone to my father. He was my brick. He always made me laugh and he taught me to not let people or situations get under my skin. With my mother no longer with us, he was my everything. We shared so much, he was still hurting over my mother's death and well I think my new life gave him entertainment in the very least. And then one day, my father asked me to go and look at a house in the village, chewing on toast I asked why?

Chapter 12

The Beach House

My father, a man who had lived such a full life already, also taught me to never give up no matter what, and that you can always survive in the most disastrous times, well basically the entire past year of my life…

Enter, my father..again, well he had always been there but this was not what I had expected to happen.

My father said that he had had enough of that family not looking after the mother of his grandchildren nor his grandchildren. So he bought a house. He moved down from the coast and originally moved into it himself for a little while. This was so exciting. This meant furniture! We would have furniture again.

The house was in the main street in the village on a long block of land with a beautiful garden filled with fruit trees, bulbs, roses, a vegetable garden and massive walnut tree up the back. The garden resembled a fairy garden that every conceivable child would dream of, running in between the trees and hedges. It was weatherboard, painted a cream colour with different levels in the smallish living area, it had big windows looking down into the garden, perfect for the cold climate as loads of sun streamed inside. It had high ceilings, only 2 bedrooms which meant that my father bought bunkbeds for the children. Actual beds again! The look on their little faces was a moment that I had to walk away down into the garden with my eyes filled with tears of joy and happiness, that I had got through the first and hardest year as a single mother, and now, I had a little help.

The children named it the Beach House, even though it was not near any beaches, it had that bright sunny feel to it. The cream, the blues inside, the atrium window over the bath where you could sit in the bath and feel like you were in the garden. It had a lovely sunny deck out the back, some of which was undercover where the previous owners had used old windows as the roof engaging the feeling of a hot house. The other part was a pergola, open area with a shade cloth for the summertime.

It had a lovely fish pond, oh dear, surely these ones would be okay? There was one large fish in it. The children named him 'Wunjo', the rune stone of joy. And yes, I had rune stones in a little basket that I used to pick one out each night after the children had gone to bed hoping that it would bring me some luck! Wunjo was enormous, definitely had been in there for a long time. The other few were normal size. We decided to get some more, naturally that turned into yet another disastrous family fish story. I mean, what else would you expect? I had an old friend who owned a large farm and was digging up a fish pond.

Enter Mr charming Land Owner of prestigious 18th century homestead, who, actually was just helping out by bringing fish for the children, however, little did I realise that he also had his sights on breaking my heart along with providing fish for the pond. We put the fish in the pond, failing to realise that the fish do not adapt from pond water to tap water and then straight back into the pond, needless to say, they were all floating sideways within 20 minutes, while my little daughters were saying "Mummy, why do they swim on their sides"….

So this exercise got a lot worse as Wunjo preceded to eat the other fish, one by one… my eldest daughter was crying at this point while I was calling out to my son, now 10, definitely the man of the house, to find a net to try to save the fish from Wunjo. This did not work as the net was too big…of course it was too big, disaster…. 3 little girls crying. I took them to the shops to buy cheesecake and icecream to try to alleviate focus on fish. Meanwhile, my son disposed of the dead fish before we returned. I am not sure how many times I paid him $5 to save whatever daily disaster we endured and to protect his sisters, but he loved it and turned that into a little business of helping mow, wash the car and watch his savings grow.

Mr charming Land Owner lasted about a day. Romantic bottle of champagne using all of his charm on his only one night date. It did not feel right. I found out the next day he was engaged to be married, pays to trust your gut feelings. This was the point I decided that I was actually okay on my own, and that he was not around long enough to gain a chapter title! Yes, the talked about pretty blonde in her silver car was now living in her father's house and had a large iron gate with my Grandfather's padlock, my brother still has today, and was happy raising my children alone, drawing support from friends around with children the same ages as mine, lighting a candle for my late mother each night with a glass of wine listening to Savage Garden songs after the children were asleep, generally cooking shortbread at 10pm when we had run out of food for school lunches the next day…

We were quite self sufficient, we had asparagus growing in the lawn, that was not intentional, we had walnuts, apricots, nectarines, peaches, apples, green gages, pumpkins, lettuces, silverbeet, figs…I was never sure what to do with figs so they all died.

Chapter 13

The Apricots

I think, by now, apart from the Applications for Property Settlement, Full Custody, Shared Care…anything in the chapter of any Family Law Textbook that I seemed to be receiving, still under constant attack legally from my ex husband, that I used to take into my great old friend's Law office to hear him say a few choice words and that he would deal with it, I was happily proving to myself that the children were going to be fine. I stopped worrying about all the bullying legal letters my ex husband and his fiancé were sending me, which, I knew was annoying them to no end, and I would attend all the sporting events alone, with a smile and morning tea packed for the children like nothing had happened. I felt I was getting myself back on my own two feet with my confidence slowly building.

If there is one thing that I hear in hurt people coming out of disastrous divorces and the like, that they might tell you they are going to destroy you, they might take everything, they might tell you you are worthless, that you are not a good parent because the fish died, not looking at the soaring certificates of great effort coming out of the school. But, destruction is a choice only you can make. I used to look him in the eye at all of the school events until he looked away. He knew I was not giving up. He still knows I will never give up. He could flash his parent's money around all the Lawyers he was engaging, most of which gave up on his attempts to destroy me, I think to date, he has had 4 or 5. Thankfully for me, the legal attempts to destroy me ended in 2012, 11 years later. That was quite an ending, one for later in the journey.

So, the Beach House had an old apricot tree, thick trunk and branches, growing next to the green gage tree. These trees flourished growing above the fish pond and this season were laden with fruit. The green gage tree, unfortunately had so much fruit it started to blow off in the wind, yes, right into the fish pond. Naturally, this course of events could only, with my luck with fish, end in a bad way. The fruit femented in the pond and finished off the remaining fish that were left in there, including Wunjo. More tears. More cheesecake, more icecream and a new copy of a favourite movie the children loved called 'The Land Before Time'.

The apricots, on the other hand became a project, when my son, during school holidays said that he was bored. I explained that he should bag up the apricots as there were so many, weigh them and sell them out the front for $2 a bag. He employed my eldest daughter, both aged about 11 and 7 at the time. I think she had to weigh them while he was up the tree and was not paid very much for doing so. I saw the big wheelbarrow disappear down the driveway covered in bags of apricots. Literally 20 minutes later my son appeared holding a tin of cash, $57 in 20 minutes. He had a grin from ear to ear. I am not sure how it became $57 not $58 considering they were $2 a bag. However, I hope the adult who ripped them of $1 thought about that later!

So the apricot business began. In a day or so there was not an apricot to be seen on the tree. My father visited with a bucket to collect some of our fine produce, only to find that my son had sold them. He laughed heartily calling my son a little so and so and was so proud of him. My son tried to give him some asparagus but my father did not like asparagus as my late mother had spent 35 years trying to force him to eat it.

The apricot business then expanded and turned into a partnership with some of our great farm friends who had a lovely, also 18th century property out at the base of the mountains and the next occurrence was a my son and their son spending hours under a shearing shed filling bags with manure and the big trailer arriving whereby we stored it in the carport and the children used to sit out with the wheelbarrow each afternoon after school selling sheep manure. The little girls became involved so the next thing was a mini market out the front of our house, plants, fruit, manure, and the youngest 2 used to find a pot and just pick a flower and stick in the pot and sell those to people driving past who just thought they were all cute children having a go at something productive. My kitchen window was at the front of the house so, rest assured, they were all well supervised! This was a great introduction I thought for teaching the children how to save money and learn to work to earn money. Sometimes it is the simple things in life which are the best and the most rewarding.

Chapter 14

The Poppy Boy

Now, this one, had I not been 7 years older than him, I could have fallen in love with. Our village and our Beach House happened to be on the artery for the greater farming area. Early 2000's was the poppy boom. Opium poppies for pharmaceutical purposes, beautiful in flower with hectares of paddocks filled with white poppies. Along with the capacity to gain contracts for such medicinal crops came a batch of strapping Field Officers who would oversee the crops and the legal boundaries for growing. Once such Field Officer walked into my old school friend's farm house one day while I was there. My friend was also a single mother and I spent an iconic summer getting together with all our small children, weekends at the beach in on a large property and at her parent's property where this Field Officer was overseeing crops.

Instant attraction, last thing I needed on my road to recovering my inner strength. It was summer, I spent the holidays at my friend's parent's house drinking cups of tea and wine with her mother, surrounded by chickens and all of our children swimming in the pool. The rest of the time I spent out beneath the mountains at my other friend's property where my daughters really learnt how to swim and dive. The Field Officer seemed to be everywhere I would be, farms, at the shop, on the road, getting a coffee.

As much as I was the devoted single mother, I was also still a living being and yes, I eventually fell into the arms of the Field Officer. That was inevitable. We single mothers are still human beings with feelings and not covered in scales as Bridget Jones put it so gallantly at the dinner party she attended in that movie. He was a lovely person. We did have a lot of fun in those 6 weeks before he left to go overseas, I let that one go. I told him he needed to meet someone who could give him a family. I was certainly not producing more babies, it was a time where 2 people met but were both on a completely different parallel in life. The day I told him and drove away I cried for weeks. I am not really sure why, I guess he was just a lovely guy and nice to my children. He gave me some element of hope that there were still nice decent men in this world.

This was the point I had accepted being alone and a strong and independent woman, but just started to wonder if this was my destiny? Did I want to be alone forever? Suddenly, I was not sure. If he had been older and perhaps in a similar situation to me, it might have worked. I am a firm believer in serendipity and fate. I believe people present in life for a reason, whether for a short time or a long time. I think he presented to show me that one day I might share my life with a nice man again who treated my children well. Just not now.

During this next phase of life at the Beach House, I continued to pour my heart and soul into raising my children, put all of my emotions on hold, did not look at any given male that I would run into, yes, I decided that was the safer option because the last thing I needed was to be hurt by some Casanova walking into our lives again, and then back out the door leaving me in tears with my wine and candle playing repeats of Savage Garden after the children were asleep, again.

I decided to buy a hammock and string it up on the pergola attached to the back of the house. Can anybody see where this story is going yet? Let me just say that hammocks seem to be on the same level as fish in my world…another epic fail. The deck and pergola seriously lent itself for a relaxing hammock to lie back in reading and I thought the children would love a little swing in it.

Quite remarkably I managed to hang the hammock to the large bolts on the pergola, the children were all watching from inside the house for safety, yes I do believe I was responsible for allocating that bad luck component. I sat in the hammock to test my masterpiece….

Bang! I hit the deck enclosed in the hammock and surrounding ropes. However, the one thing that I did assume in an accurate manner was the attachment of the ropes to the large pergola bolts, which, then, before I could move, caused the large planks of pergola to rip from the house all falling around and upon myself. My son was shaking his head from inside the house. The little girls were all laughing and clapping at their mother as I believe they thought I was performing some sort of entertainment for them.

My father called that afternoon asking how my day had been. As I looked out at the pile of the actual back part of the house I responded with, "oh Dad, just a normal day here". Thankfully he was too busy to visit for a few days which gave me time to have tradesmen fix the pergola. I never told my father that story, nor the one where I had tried to paint the hallway ceiling but failed to buy ceiling paint so ended up white as the paint all dripped down on myself, the tarp and most of the carpet at the time.

Life went on, the legal letters still flowed in every few months and they did not frighten me anymore surprisingly. I had proved myself to the community that I was coping as a single mother and had nothing short of adoration and encouragement from friends and so many people in the village. People started to realise my story, they watched my ex husband, his and his fiance's lifestyle compared to mine with the children.

When it came to holidays, the children and I used to travel in the tiny silver car to the beach, we had the use of a 'shack', as we call a simple beach house in Australia, which was called "The Tin Shed" and belonged to family friends. It was a few rooms built off the back of a machinery shed on a 5000 acre sheep and cattle property on the island. It was tiny, the little girls and I had to sleep in one bed and my son and eldest daughter had the single beds in the spare bedroom. It had a fireplace and tiny living area, very outdated carpet and looked out over the paddocks beyond the long line of pine trees that disappeared toward the coastline.

The Tin Shed was where I found so much peace. The only sounds I could hear at night after our cosy nights watching movies, eating chocolate, when the children would be asleep, and the fire had turned to smoulders, was the sea air blowing peacefully or some nights furiously across the plains, and, in particular the sound of the wind in the pine trees, the odd sounds of sheep and cattle in the distance. There was a wooden seat outside and I used to sit out there and embrace the tranquility.

This was the time that I started to learn to let go, to let go of the negative legal letters, the negative visits from my ex husband collecting or returning the children as he oftened yelled at me in an intimidating and degrading manner, the condescending smiles from his fiancé sitting up in the car. As much as I still had to deal with the negative, their games, their attempts to sway the children with money and sheer bribery, I chose peace.

I stood out there in the wind that night and threw my wedding ring out onto the plains. The feeling of power came back into my heart. He was not going to destroy me. His fiancé and her sarcastic smiles were not going to intimidate me. I knew the children and I would be alright. I knew I could conquer this situation, finally, I held some inches of hope that life would become easier again. The stars shone above the pine trees, it was a clear night and all I could hear was the wind blowing. The power within to let go is as deep as any belief will allow, it is healing, it is a power to not let negativity consume your soul. Once you can learn to block negative, only see positive, you will be surprised what can transpire.

Chapter 15

The Estate

I t is universally known that when times are the darkest and often most difficult, it is a time where the light is not that far away.

This was almost the case for me, well, for a little while…

I heard that a local country historic estate needed tour guides so I put up my hand to be considered. All my children were in school now and I had some spare time during the day, after dropping my youngest daughter to the kindergarten and then literally run out the door before she noticed that I was gone, a difficult time for sure! Then I had to run across the grassed area and jump over the fence so she did not see me disappear up the path… At this point I would be the mother crying in the car!

I became a tour guide in this idealistic and beautiful 18th century estate which overlooked the river and was just outside the village. I learnt a lot about the history and enjoyed the time to myself during the day. I was then offered the office position and, before long I was upholding running the entire estate, accommodation cottages, restaurant, house and garden tours, maintenance and events. This helped my confidence in extremes! It flowed into helping our Accountant with the books and eventually I turned a not for profit organisation into one that had a $45,000 profit one year whereby we had money to spend on maintaining the old buildings without applying for Government grants.

It was a fun time. I held a successful human resources attitude and every staff member seemed content. Naturally, somebody on the Board of Directors decided that we were doing so well that we should hire a General Manager from a casino background.

Enter..Mr Casino with his groomed wet look hair and shiny suit.. For some reason, I had the feeling that this would be the beginning of the end of my career at this lovely estate, and notoriously yes, I was right. Mr Casino had absolutely no farm experience, milked me for knowledge and then discarded me for all of the board meetings, presenting all of my advertising and marketing ideas as his own.

He discovered I was a single mother from the village and obviously worked out that I was potentially vulnerable, especially now being his direct employee. So he asked me to stay late one night and brought in a beer to my desk. He then tried to massage my shoulders telling me how I had done such a great job that day. This then evolved into telling me how beautiful I was and that he was attracted to me…oh goodness, here goes my career I thought…

Mr Casino in his shiny suit was also married.

I resisted his moves. The next morning I received a written warning for my position, explaining that I was not 'performing' to standards that he expected as my boss. I showed it to some of my staff in disbelief and told them that that was it, I was not being treated like that and I was going to confront him. One of my tour guides said "Oh but Katerina, you know what he is like, you will lose your job", as I stormed into his office.

I mustered all the courage after being intimidated by my ex husband, the School Teacher, the Land Owner and threw his written warning on his desk and told him he was nothing but a cheap sleaze and he could stick his job. I walked out. He started to chase me out the door, knowing that he could not do the job without me, I kept on going down the dirt driveway beside the river. The Head Groundsman, who happened to also be my children's taekwondo instructor, grabbed Mr Casino and said, "Let her go, unless you want me to walk as well and probably everybody else".

So that was the sad ending to a lovely position I had at the historic estate. Needless to say that Mr Casino is also no longer there, and his wife left him. Karma does come back to haunt some people who mistreat others at times.

I went home and had a glass of wine with tears in my eyes looking up into our lovely little garden, my home, my safe haven, nobody could hurt me here. And then I got on with life with the children and put the estate in the archive's department of my thoughts.

While I was working at the Estate, a few of my staff included me in the social life of the village and, in particular, the local football club. So, suddenly, on the weekends the children were at the farm, I had invitations to attend functions at the clubrooms.

Well, this was a lot of fun at first to feel like I belonged out socially. However, I did not see this one coming…

Chapter 16
The Footballer

Enter Mr Footballer…and my first experience with domestic violence. Of course he was charming, to be honest I did not really find him terribly attractive, but, having been alone for so long it was nice to have somebody in my life. There was a lot of hype being a footballer's girlfriend as we were all treated so well by the club and you almost felt like a bit of a celebrity getting all dressed up for the functions. I did not really involve him with the children, he did meet them but I think, deep down, I knew that he would not be around for long! Eight months this one lasted, oh goodness, by the end of it that was certainly enough.

I have little to say about him as a person really. He was a farm hand on a friend's property, a few years younger than I. I met his family once, where his younger brother let it slip that his other girlfriend was there last weekend. Seriously, where do I find these men? I was on a winner here…not…

So I called the relationship off, domestic violence unaware of how these perpetrators work in their sick and twisted minds. He threw a beer in my eyes at the football club. I left and walked home. Of course he followed and I was physically abused at my own house. He threw me around the living room like I was a rag doll, bruised my body but did not touch my face. I have since learnt from Counsellors that a lot of the worst perpetrators injure the body not the face so they can isolate their victim and nobody knows. He smashed my phone and pulled the internet cords from the wall. Then he left telling me he was not finished with me. I padlocked the gate that night, and every night following.

If there is one thing I can tell you in my experience, is if you find yourself in this predicament, please seek help from the Police as soon as this happens. The system is in place for good reason, to protect. I was not really sure what to do as I was physically hurt, emotionally crushed and had lost the safe factor at my own home. It is normal to feel like this. It is also common for the experience to not be over on the first occasion too, so as much as I can say that if it happens to you to seek help immediately, I did not. There is only one person who can say that they are ready to escape this type of situation, and that is yourself, hence hearing of many women and men who continue being abused both mentally and physically and sometimes the perpetrator will wear them down to the point of losing weight, confidence, hope and faith.

So this man was openly seen our in public with his 'other' girlfriend and I became a hermit. I was too scared to go to the football club to see my new friends, too scared to go out at all, so when the children were at the farm I would not leave the house, I would sit in the dark hiding at night waiting for his usual tormenting. He did not try to see me, he would stop outside and ring the doorbell constantly, he would bang his fists on the windows, he even broke a window one night. Thankfully he never attempted any of this while the children were home. I ended up getting a screw driver and pulling the doorbell to pieces, that ended up in the kitchen drawer, along with everything else that failed to work and I could not fix.

Then there was the night that was the decider for me to act and contact the Police.

I had gone to a friend's house and there were a few people there having a barbeque. He walked in uninvited, unannounced and threw a glass of beer in my eyes again…Let me tell you it blinds you for a few minutes, not recommended at all!! He grabbed my phone and left. Instead of making a good decision and just calling the Police, I decided to follow him to his house on a farm down the road to plead with him to give me my phone back. All I could think of at the time was my ex husband trying to contact me about the children and I did not have my phone. I did not consider my own dangerous position once…until he opened the door of his house, which, was approximately 1 kilometre from any other house… terrible decision on my part. At some point in our life we make a stupid decision, this was my moment…

This night was nothing short of horrific. Firstly, he threw my car keys on his roof. Now I knew I was not safe at all. I could see the lights of the big farm house in the distance but there was no way that I could get their attention. This man pulled me inside his house and threw me around again, hitting, kicking, slapping my face, pulling my hair, he threw me across a wood heater so I had burns to my hands, it went on and on. The anger in his eyes was terrifying.

Then, after he raped me, he did that Karate Kid 'sweep the leg' move on my knee and left me curled up with my knee cap moved on my leg.

I was dragged into a spare room and he shut the door and left me in there. I honestly thought I was going to be killed. Then I heard him snoring, after what seemed like hours, so I snuck out of the room. I tip toed across the living area floor and noticed that he had retrieved my car keys from the roof and left them near the door. I picked them up and left the house. Of course the sliding door to the outside squeaked but I thought I was clear. It was winter so it was icy outside on the driveway, especially without shoes on, yes he had thrown those on the roof too.

I limped down the gravel driveway towards my car crying silently. It was around 4am. This ordeal had gone on since around 10pm the night before. I was so sore. I was exhausted, dehydrated, shaking uncontrollably. And then I heard him storm out of the house, my knee was so sore that I could not put any real weight on it to go any faster. He grabbed me and tossed me into a fireman's lift dragging me back to the house, I was crying uncontrollably as my face dragged grazing in the gravel. I pleaded that he let me try to walk. He did. He was next to me. I was wearing a ring on my right hand with a decent size stone in it. He started saying he was sorry, another common habit of these perpetrators, I cried some more to gain his pity as I thought this might be my chance to make him stop hurting me; and then, deep down, I felt a sudden urge of strength within me and I had no idea where it came from. I stood on my working leg and backhanded him fair in the face, which, wearing this lovely large stone on my ring caused him enough bleeding and pain to double over long enough for me to get in my car and lock the doors.

He was yelling at me and started kicking my car as my shaking hand managed to start the engine, he jumped on the bonnet of the car trying to stop me from leaving, I suddenly accelerated then stopped so he fell off the car, I reversed as he was getting up from the ground and, as tempting as it was to drive into him, I drove around him and left him standing in a cloud of dust. I was driving down the long gravel driveway looking in my rear mirror hoping that I could get as far down the road as possible so he could not find me. I made it home. As the sun rose on a quiet, foggy Sunday morning, I parked my car hidden from the road up in the garden and padlocked the gate. I called one of my friends who came straight over. I reported him to the Police. They drove out there and arrested him.

To this day, my children, until they read this book, do not know of this night. My ex husband never knew either. As far as he was ever concerned I had failed an 8 month relationship and he and his fiancé told everybody they knew in the village that apparently I failed at all my relationships. I think this one had been worthy of failure? The Footballer was not allowed anywhere near me, my children or my house. He came to say goodbye after he had been fired from his job, had endured a couple of punch-ups at the football club when they found out what he had done to me and I had heard he was moving interstate. I went out the front of my house. He said that he was sorry for what he did. I picked up the closest large terracotta pot plant that I could carry and threw it at his ute and told him to not ever come back. Of course there was potting mix all over the road and chunks of terracotta. Luckily for him, I was not strong enough to actually hit the ute, it clipped the edge of the bumper bar but that was enough to send him running.

Moving forward, that was the last I ever saw of him. The moral of this chapter, is to not put yourself in a dangerous situation. Trust the authorities and what they are trained to do, and dodge hot woodheaters, as they really do hurt.

In amongst losing a job I really liked and getting rid of a boyfriend I did not really like at all, the children's father announced the date of his wedding. Great, just as my life looked about as unbalanced personally than ever, I had their wedding news splashed all over the village, how wonderful it was going to be, how lovely the marquee would be… etc..etc..Suddenly I did feel like the next Bridget Jones. I even checked if I did have scales forming, no..oh that was a good outcome! His fiancé would come to my house all smiles, and I would just smile back at them, all sarcastically on their part. I am not sure why she honestly thought I cared about their wedding, I did not care at all as long as the children were looked after at the farm.

I think I just felt like surely it was my turn for a little goodluck, or something you read of in books! I used to be expected to supply all the clothes for when the children went to the farm, a lot of which were ruined by mud and farm games, which, I did not mind but I knew they had old farm clothes over there and had no idea why they would let the children ruin the clothes I provided? I began thinking it was a little vindictive…especially when I collected 36 of the girl's jumpers that miraculously had a definite v-shaped tear in the front. I put them all in a garbage bag and gave them to the children's father one day and he asked why. I was stronger now and spoke my mind a lot more and I simply said that they need replacing and that the holes were only in the front?! He then said, "are you saying that my fiancé has cut holes in the jumpers?"….I laughed and said, "You said it not me"…

So the wedding came around and the girls were to be flower girls. I sat down one night and thought to myself of all the ruined jumpers, months of no child support, the car being taken, being left with $3.52, his fiancé yelling at me in the street and I decided, a week before the wedding that my girl's needed their hair trimmed. I am sure you can all see where this is going. I lined them up and asked if they wanted their hair trimmed, knowing that a couple of the little girls at school had recently had their long hair lopped off into cute little bob styles about collar length. Smiling to myself, away I went after the girls told me they wanted their hair short like their friends.

The look on the faces of both the children's father and his fiancé was priceless when they came all smiling in their intimidating manner towards me as usual. They said in unison, "you cut their hair?"…to which I replied, "Yes, I did". I turned on one foot and waved to them smiling and went inside. I closed the door and jumped up saying "YES!" Finally I had the gumption to have a little go back!

Chapter 17
The Apartment

A very positive event transpired from this Domestic Violence occurrence, would anyone ever believe? It made me feel a lot stronger in time, not straight away of course, but with the help of qualified Counsellors and hours of trying to piece together why… There was not really a lot that I had not dealt with this far as a single parent. In reflection, I had been stripped of basically most of the children's and my belongings, had experienced having no money, had lost a car, crashed 2 others, had had an unhappy marriage, a couple of short useless flings, a sleazy boss and been beaten by another man. I think that is enough to warrant standing up for myself, which I did! Surprisingly I was happy, possibly the happiest I had been for years, the children were all happy which was my main focus but I was happily coasting along on this strange path of survival!

My father had decided to open a Real Estate Office in the city. He offered me the full time position of Office Manager. He also said he felt it was time to move a little further away from the children's father, his wife and all the family driving past our house. The office was located right in the central business district of the city, how exciting I thought! I spoke to the children about this idea. It was always my priority to speak to the children as we were a tight knit little unit now. They were keen to move as there was so many different activities living in the city than in the village. So it was settled, we were to move.

Standing up for myself….yes, I had to tell the children's father that we were moving away. Of course he organised an intimidating legal letter with a half mast attempt at filing an Application for Full Custody of the children. I had learnt such a lot about the Laws and was not the least bit worried as he had agreed for me being the Primary Carer years before, he obviously forgot that part…

So I told him face to face at the car. He was furious. I simply explained that there were so many more educational opportunities in the city as the children were growing up and that the city was only 20 minutes drive so I was not restricting his visitation rights. Boom, he had no comeback. I had become stronger!

We moved to the city. I thought this was a good balance for the children in any case as they had the farm with their father and then city with me.

The apartment life was a few years we just loved. It was right in the main street, an old building with a renovated apartment above, high ceilings, polished timber floors, huge rooms and a lovely big deck up in the rooftops protected by a modern glass fence. The entire front part was windows which looked out over the rooftops of the city.

The children would go off to school and I could work downstairs for my father. It stopped all the legal letters from the children's father, it stopped him sending the Police if I was 5 minutes late getting home from work, yet he and his mother would never offer to help out and babysit so I could work and pay for everything. Suddenly, my father was my buffer again and the children were all in the building. They loved it as we had access to the printers and 7 computers for their homework and projects at school! There were no more arguments about who was using the computer. Their father backed off again from he and his wife's constant obsession in trying to prove I was not a good mother.

Office hours were often interesting. I remember being with one of our Landlords we acted on behalf of in the Property Management Office and it was a student free day at the school so the children were all upstairs. We had a staircase that came down the back of the building so the children were able to come and see me at any given point of the day, a perfect set up really to be able to juggle work and children as a single parent. I was speaking to this Landlord and noticed a rope hanging down the window outside coming from my youngest daughter's bedroom. As it came down, there were teddy bears and dolls tied to the rope. The Landlord said,

"That is interesting, I do not think I have seen that before while discussing my properties., to which I replied, "Student free day…". She laughed and most of our regular clients knew we lived upstairs so they were accustomed to locating the odd toy in the office and two cats, one of which would sit at the table next to my father while he signed Contracts with clients. Point being, this was my life, juggling. Juggling all these little balls up in the air, wondering which one was going to land alright and which next disaster or challenge would occur and when… it was never 'if' the next anything would occur, always when. This particular student free day was no surprise either. I was working away on the advertising when I heard an extremely large crash from above. A couple of our sales staff offered to watch reception while I went up the back stairs to the apartment to see what had happened.

Glass everywhere. Middle daughter crying and laughing at the same time. Of course she had skidded on the polished floors and managed somehow, I am still not sure if I ever got the entire story, to ended up going through the glass coffee table. The others did not elaborate any further and fortunately apart from some cuts she was okay. I looked at all their little faces halfway knowing that I did not have the full story of how she ended up through the table with this amount of force but went back downstairs to work.

The children were all growing by now so there were different issues, like the odd taekwondo fight that smashed something, sporting injuries, cooking disasters, stolen bikes that had not been locked up, lost shoes, lost socks, a surfboard through one of the kitchen windows…there was never a dull moment! One day my son tied one to a bed with her hands behind her back and his underpants on her head. We had grazed knees from roller blading up the street to the city park, I would count heads when they would be home from school in case one of them had missed the bus, which, inevitably did happen some days.

In amongst all of this, our black male cat would stop all of the city traffic by sitting in the middle of the road. He also was found at the Sunday school across the road. I bought him a tag with my phone number on it so that became the city hotline as there were no cats in the city, except ours. People would call at any hour saying they had seen our 2 cats wherever. The other tabby and white cat used to visit the Italian restaurant next door and sit at their bar. She loved a gift shop and was locked in there one night. I went for a walk and saw her in the window. My life was a great big puzzle of dealing with work, 4 growing children, 2 cats and 1 son, now a teenager.

Teenage boys. Thankfully he had lovely friends in secondary school. I still think they are lovely, even after some of the boyish stupid events they created. They constructed a potato launcher. If any of you do not know, this is basically a gun fuelled by hairspray and a match and poly pipes from the hardware store. I wondered for quite some time where my hairspray was going so quickly…and then the potatoes were disappearing by the bag full. Then I caught them, all laughing firing potatoes against the carpark wall.

I did receive a phone call one day asking if I was the mother of the boy aiming a gun out of the front window of the apartment across the street…I tried to say no but the man said he had seen me there so that did not work. I apologised and said that it would not happen again that my son would be firing potatoes across the road at peak hour trying to hit a pole on the other side. There were so many similar stories of childhood fun that I dealt with, things that would have been easier to deal with not being the only parent dealing with them, and, of course their father would not help out, so I could not call him for support at all because then he would try taking me to Court again over something!? Needless to say, there was never a dull moment.

We had a stairwell down onto the main street. Normally we never used this front entrance as it needed a key. To be honest, I do not think I have ever locked any of our houses that had the option. There were just too many of us coming and going with the 4 children and I seemed to inherit all of their friends most of the time as well. There were never enough keys in any case, and generally somebody was home or close to being home. With the combination of taekwondo uniforms and potato guns coming and going, I think half the city thought we were a little crazy and probably would not dare to try and break in. Not only that, I always made a nice home, one that looked homely and inviting, but, the reality was, there was mostly nothing of any value for anybody to steal apart from the food in the fridge.

I was at work one day and my son decided to lock his sisters in the stairwell. This event they videoed and it was just priceless. It was also a very powerful lesson to all the parents who supply screen after screen to their children, for holiday entertainment. Because of our situation, we only had one computer, the children eventually got phones as they got older but they were still children creating fun out of their imagination, whether on bikes, skateboards, firing potatoes at a wall or locking each other in the stairwell giving the others a chance to escape by trying to reach the key with a coat hanger. This video I would love to play today, however, of course the computer blew up eventually and we lost all that was on there… I had never heard you had to back up files?! Another manual in life that I missed.

The city life for these country children was always eventful. They were used to the open spaces so did not bother with how they looked at times. My youngest daughter I asked to go down to buy a newspaper at the newsagent which, I might add was in the busiest street in the city. I asked my middle daughter what the little one was wearing on her very independent trip approximately 50 metres to run this errand. "Pyjamas and ugg boots Mum", my middle daughter replied. Of course she was, I thought, hoping that nobody we knew happened to see her. But this was my life. There was so much going on that it was easy to miss just one little detail so easily. I basically needed a separate set of eyes per child.

I think the point here is being a single parent you do not have any assistance, particularly without huge family support and when you combine that with a lot of children, there are going to be things that you just plainly miss. My children were great children, all very strong, centred and excelling in school even amongst their dysfunctional home life. It had become time for my son to learn to drive. Dear God….and I had 4 of them. Plus I was notoriously bad at reversing a motor vehicle myself. My son was in the passenger seat as we were talking about him starting to drive and I was explaining that it does come to you with practice, as I drove down our driveway to park and straight into the fence. The side mirror fell off so I just picked it up while he was uncontrollably laughing and put it in the kitchen drawer. The kitchen drawer…you really needed a passport to enter that drawer. Most disasters ended up in there, including the cat one night for the whole night. We were wondering where the poor little darling had gone.

So we all survived the Apartment days. I used to once again, sit out on the deck looking out across the rooftops at night after the children had gone to bed appreciating every ounce of laughter of that house, enjoying my wine and candle for my mother. I had really embraced being single and actually happy. It really was where financially we were coping as I was working full time while juggling this array of sporting events, soccer balls, taekwondo events, bikes, friends, up to 5 on a weekend for sleepovers.

My father decided to sell the real estate office so I worked for another company. An old colleague I used to work with in hairdressing years before was also working there. She asked me to join her and her partner, who happened to be a Managing Partner in a local Law Firm for drinks. About 3 wines down we decided to open our own hairdressing salon in the back of an old friend's music shop in the centre of the city. We managed to convince the bank to give us an overdraft. Still, to this day I think it was merely our looks that got us that overdraft, it worked in any case. The music shop had a café and we built a salon from scratch at the back.

That year was a lot of fun. The music shop was the hub of the city and we knew enough people to make this business work. We had clients streaming in, we never started until 9:30am and usually finished at 3:00pm! But then our clients started bringing bottles of wine to their appointments so naturally we had most of the morning free and were constantly busy in the afternoons. I guess you could say it was a bit of a solace of reprieve for mothers and became the 'Bad Mom's'[3] salon like the movie! Suddenly I had some freedom of choice and it opened my mind to the thought that there were things that a single parent left with 4 children and $3.52 could achieve.

In amongst the salon days and the children all coasting along well at school, naturally my glasses became foggy again when Mr Ralph Lauren came in for a haircut. This was a bullet I should have dodged right from the start I can assure you but I miraculously turned to mush at the charming well dressed man who seemed to say everything right. He started coming into the salon pursuing me every day and eventually after a large bunch of flowers and about 2 haircuts a week, I agreed to a date. I still remember he took me to the movies and tried to hide me from

---

[3] *Bad Moms,* STX Entertainment, H.Brothers, Tang Media Productions, (2016).

his ex girlfriend, that I found out later had just dumped him so he was looking for somewhere to live. She was also a client at our salon which was awkward in itself.

He took me to see the movie 'He's just not that into you'….surely I was not this stupid. Oh yes I was. Talking about signs, I should have seen this massive lighthouse beaming in front of me…

Chapter 18
The 'Serial Killer'

Before I continue, please understand that this particular well dressed creep was not an actual murderer, however, he did prove to pertain to some thoughts that were just weird and somewhat unstable. My younger children decided he was to be known jokingly as 'The Serial Killer'.

Mr charming Ralph Lauren type well dressed…man…human, I still cannot find the right words for him really, decided after two dates to leave his bike at our Apartment. He seemed to think that our surname meant that I was rich, I guess, being a salon owner I could have been, had we not opened it up on a massive overdraft and were in debt up to our eyeballs, that and our surname was far from the term rich, well the family were, I was still building on the $3.52 and maintaining schooling costs and trying to keep my beat up motor vehicle running. A few days later this charmer seemed to have moved his clothes into our home. My middle daughter rang me at the salon to ask if he was moving in. I said that I had not discussed it with him but she assured me he was already there with his feet up watching television. Oh dear…

This was quite confusing. What was I to do here? Most girls dream of having a bunch of flowers shining in the kitchen and a well dressed, great career type guy without an ex wife or children to accommodate living in your home. And, it appeared he, with all of those credentials was sitting on my couch.

Suddenly my single life spending my nights with my wine and my candle looking over the rooftops on the deck were gone. I missed my single life. He did move in, well he already had without asking or discussing the option. He took me shopping and bought me an entire wardrobe of designer clothing brands, made me try them all on in a changeroom flashing his credit card around and also chatting up the store staff. It was similar to that scene in the movie 'Pretty Woman'[4], except this guy was not legitimate.

Long story short we ended up leaving our beloved Apartment to go a little further down the road to an old terrace house because it had become a little cramped with him living with us, all his idea really. I actually would not have minded if he left. I let him start controlling me. Amazing how easily this can happen to a girl when you think and really know you are stronger that that. But you still let him in …for a while anyway. So he was there all the time. In the house he ate all the food, did not help out financially, took up the entire couch so the children sat on the floor. At first he was nice to them and to me. Then the signs became clearer and clearer that he was your classic narcissist.

When the children were out at the farm I would stay in the salon until late to avoid being home with him. He told my middle daughter after a few months that when he was finished with me that he would chop me up and put me in the woodfire. That was the moment I knew that I had a huge problem on my hands. Even the footballer who did those dreadful things to me had not ever said words to that effect.

He would watch girls on the television and tell me I should lose weight, even though I was an average weight, he would tell me my eye makeup was wrong when we would go out with his friends, he did not like my hair, my shoes, in the end my children, he did not like my cushions, told me to sell my car but I did not. I knew that he was sleeping with other women. Come on guys…if you expect your girlfriend to wash the lipstick off your collar, trust that we know. We are basically like beagle dogs and can sniff trouble! Finally he asked to upload photos on our computer as he did not know how. At this point I was beginning to despise this man and wondering how I was going to remove him from our home, and safely I might add because he was becoming quite nosy in my salon business and aggressive in the way he treated me.

I told him that I would need his password to access his Facebook account not thinking that he would actually be stupid enough to give it to me. He was…bingo, I was in. I showed him innocently how to upload photos and waited patiently until the next day to be able to look at this account and find out whose lipstick he had been wearing on his clothes.

Classic moment. Poured a glass of champagne, found out he was not going to be home for a while and logged in. It turned out he had 6 women on the go…and myself.. busy guy…. He had his active status on so at one point while I was reading all the flirty booty call conversations about how great their sex lives were, all 6 of them, 1 of them wrote "Hey baby I missed you today", oh dear, now what was I meant to do? Reply of course!!! I never loved this man so this

---

[4] *Pretty Woman,* Touchstone Pictures, Silverscreen Partners IV, Regency International Pictures, (1990).

was all quite easy for me to turn the whole relationship into a total disaster. Plus he had taken us away from our beloved Apartment and put us in this daggy old terrace with terrible curtains and bad green carpet. I did have to be careful though. After the footballer I could sense the aggression factor.

So I ended up having a chat with all 6 of these girls and promised that he would see them all tomorrow. Okay, doing that, I knew that his day was to be the breakup day because as soon as they were all angry at him I would be busted. The girls were going out to the farm that night and my son, now 17, to a friend's house, well at that age they are basically everywhere, driving and independent. Perfect night to get rid of the Serial Killer, I thought. I had organised drinks with 2 friends after work so I had a chance to tell them and ask their advice on the breakup I had planned, as you do, when you need to run these things around a table and champagne before you make a life changing decision. I told him an hour later we were meeting to give me time to talk to them.

He arrived early. He had become obsessed with me being in public without him. That, in itself was a huge beacon alarm bell! So we endured drinks. My friends could sense I was not right. I could not express that though so it was all just uncomfortable. Finally we left. The taxi driver dropped us off. I had managed to not drink very much because I just had a very dark feeling about the evening. I was right. Always trust you gut feelings is what I say. Always. Never ever doubt them.

We arrived home and the house appeared empty. He grabbed me. Oh here we go. He started telling me that I was an embarrassment to be around because apparently I had been a bit quiet at drinks. I just pulled away from him and said that maybe he should be asking his 6 other girls why I might not be excited to be out having drinks with him…. I was done. This was it. The breakup was about to happen and I was not going to back down and let this go on any longer in my life. I knew by the look in his eyes I was about to be hurt physically, oh dear God, not again. I remember thinking to stay away from the woodfire. It is not a nice feeling knowing that a 6ft 2" man is about to beat the living daylights out of your poor little 5ft 5" body.

Here we go, be prepared I thought as he pushed me backwards towards the bedroom and through the door with me hitting the door. He whacked me with both palms in the chestplate which, I did not realise at the time he had fractured. This time during the ordeal of being punched in the face over and over, strangled until I was seeing stars I remember thinking we are in the middle of the city, surely he will not kill me. Then I heard a large thud of a chair being moved upstairs, my son was home. I called out, he had obviously heard this man yelling as he beat me. My son literally flew down the stairs it seemed so fast and pulled this man off me by his shirt.

This man tried to strangle my son and his fingernails dug into my son's neck and scratched badly as my son pushed him away. My son called his best friend and this perpetrator realised he could be in trouble with the law so he sat on the couch while my son held a baseball bat calling the Police. At this point I was crying in the arms of my son's friend until the Police arrived. Naturally the serial killer as we came to know him tried to run away knocking my son into the garden on his way out the door knowing the Police were on their way.

My son's friend and myself ran to the gate and, in a terrified yet closure type moment, I hurled a lump of firewood down the street at the serial killer yelling for him to never come back! This piece of wood seemed to be airborn for what seemed like forever, my son's friend even commented "oh dear I hope that doesn't hit him and kill him!", jokingly, but with my injuries, halfway not! Thankfully, he did not get knocked out by a piece of firewood and by then we entertained the fact that the Police had arrived so we knew it was over. My son was out of the garden and okay, scratched by roses but in good shape. What a night…

Moral of that story…do not continue going out with a man who tells your primary school aged daughter that when he would be finished with me that he would chop me up and put me in the woodheater. Moral of that story for him, he wound up charged by the Police with 2 counts of Common Assault, lost his job and his ability to ever work around minors again and a large fine. The footballer had got away with this type of pathetic behaviour more than once so at least I had learnt from that to call the authorities the first time and trust their judgment and protection.

If there is anything I can pass on to you as readers, it is, that this type of abuse is not okay, it can damage you for years mentally, the physical hurt is just a reminder of past injuries that I am still reminded of when I try to run or lift something or hold my arms up for a while, but the damage it causes to your confidence is the worst kind, the kind you can work through with the proper counselling avenues. The main point being that you can get your life back, your safe life, and, you do not need to put up with this treatment forever. We are worth more that that.

So, from hereon, in that house, I lived in fear. I grew to hate that house. Every day a memory of that wretched night. Because this man had been charged accordingly, I half expected that he would return. My son thought of something very smart as we knew that the serial killer man knew that my bedroom window did not have a lock on it and it was on the ground floor at the front of the house. Even charged, sometimes these kind of perpetrators do try to come back so they can be all sweet and lovely professing their love for you for the only reason that you might drop all charges and then be back to square one….to only be beaten again in time as they tend not to change.

I moved to the top level of the house. My son moved to the front bedroom. I did notice that his friends stayed a lot during these months with the Court date pending. They all slept on the floor in his bedroom. It was as if they knew that this man would be back. I knew my daughters would be safe as this perpetrator was smart enough to realise that any more charges might land him in jail, and, a pretty boy like himself having hurt a minor had watched enough movies to know that jail may not be the right place for him.

So the backdoor had never locked and the serial killer had known that. I am not sure why every house I seemed to have moved my children into had doors that did not lock properly. My son had managed to make the door lockable. This felt safer.

And then the night happened. I really do not think I had ever felt such fear as hearing somebody trying to open the back door. The children were all asleep as it was a school night and my new bedroom happened to be right above the back door below. I froze. It was 11:30pm. All the lights were out. I lay there listening to the door handle jiggle. I knew it was him, recognised his overly confident march up the back stairs. I peeped out from behind the blinds and saw him trying to jiggle the window into the kitchen which we had jammed closed with wood so it was not able to be opened. I did not want to call the Police as my window was open upstairs and I thought he might hear me and break the window. The only other window was the one downstairs into my son's bedroom at the front. My heart was racing so much I thought it was about to jump out of my body. I grabbed the baseball bat from the cupboard. I had turned into a bird that was about to swoop anything that endangered my babies. That was all of which I could think. I saw him proceed to the front of the house. I crept down the stairs, baseball bat in hand in the dark. My son was asleep in the front room. I saw his shadow at the front window. No. This was not going to happen. I was not going to let this man climb through my son's window and scare the daylights out of him. It had been my fault that I went out with this lunatic so I would handle it, thought with all the confidence of Cinderella not Rambo.

My next move was potentially one of the most stupid and unsafe moves any girl, particularly a physically injured one could undertake. This is not recommended to any female in this situation at all. However, it remarkably worked and I am still alive. I carefully opened the front door, which was a silent door, I had worked that out. The woodpile was right at the door which was set back under a mini verandah. I could hear him starting to fiddle with the front window. I picked up a big piece of firewood and stepped out and threw it at him saying, "Buggar off". Well, he looked in complete fear and ran away. I jumped back inside holding my baseball bat and shut the door. I sat at the front door on the floor startled for quite some time in the dark. I then checked all the windows again. I did not sleep that night. I drank the rest of last night's wine sitting next to the woodheater staring at the flames, in fear, in the dark.

The next morning I said to the children as we all got ready for the day and none of them knew what had happened, while they slept and their mother had acted in her own James Bond movie, that we should move house. They all agreed that they did not like the deck, the curtains, the carpet, a whole list came out of them! I think, basically, they did not like this house as it reminded them, as with me, of the serial killer man. That was it. We needed a new start.

Before we left that house we held a farewell for my son as he embarked on going to the mainland for a career. We decided to have a party with about 20 of his friends and their parents. I have to say that this whole idea was such fun. We had never had a party. I did not realise that this would entail what it did.

We had a barbeque on the deck and naturally my father was in charge of cooking. The teenagers were all behaving well down in the garden and the parents all seemed to be having a nice time. And then suddenly my father, who was cooking with my great Lawyer friend who had handled my divorce asked the last time I had cleaned out the fat tray in the barbeque that I had had for approximately 2 years. I had no idea you had to do that.

This, obviously resulted in a barbeque fire which smoked out the entire garden and neighbouring gardens, blackened the whole cream coloured wall of the house and resulted in my Lawyer friend picking up one of pot plants and throwing it at the barbeque so we ended up in a big pile of potting mix, no meat and just salad for dinner. The night went on and one of the boys accidentally threw a bottle over the fence which sailed through the neighbour's window so they called the Police who arrived to see the marinated chicken covered in potting mix and all the guests smelt of wood smoke. The Police Officer's children were student's in my son's taekwondo class thankfully so there were no problems. My father poured himself another glass of red wine laughing saying that this was a great party…I just looked at him.

The clean up was fun. It had rained overnight so the potting mix had turned to mud. The remainder of the salads were filled with water and half of the lettuce had washed out onto the deck combining with the sausages, chicken, steak, all coated in mud. Instead of a simple wash of the dishes, this clean up needed, a shovel, a wheelie bin and a garden hose.

So, a milestone of first child leaving home….potting mix chicken garnished with garlic and basil, floating salad in a combination of balsamic dressing and rain, mud on deck, barbeque to be taken away and one black wall home seemed perfect of a historic terrace house. Excellent moment as a single parent.

Chapter 19
"Our" Street

There was a Georgian cottage further up the hill, actually built on the side of the hill, overlooking the city that became available to rent. My son had left the state so it was just the girls and I. This little home seemed perfect for us. I needed to feel safe, especially since my son had gone. There was only the front door and two windows on the road and the rest of the house was built into the hill so it ticked all the boxes of privacy and safety.

I had had to sell the salon. My business partner had been diagnosed with secondary cancer and during the trials and tribulations of the serial killer man, had been having treatment. It broke my heart the wintery day I met her for coffee at a quirky little café on the hill near a large park with one hundred year old trees and she was yellow. She sat looking at me through her yellow eyes telling me to not accept any bad men anymore. I gave her a hug as we parted and watched her drive away. I sat on the bonnet of my car looking across the park watching the autumn leaves fall from the trees in each breath of wind wondering about life really. My business partner passed away 6 days later. That had been the last day I saw her.

So there I was…no salon and three daughters at school. The fridge was empty..again. Naturally my ex husband was still creatively accounting his finances and paying the minimum child support amount while buying children's friend's unnecessarily expensive birthday presents and billing me without my consent. I could never really get my head around why his wife would pay me the minute monthly amount that half the time I would not receive and had to call him asking for her cheque, only to be told she had left it in the car…the car..yes the one he had taken from his children and their mother and put her and her children in…thank goodness I managed to let all of that go realising how stupid it was.

So my business partner's partner was still at the law firm and gave me a job. They needed a receptionist so I bought a suit and this was my entry into law. I began my very corporate career. There were so many balls all flying around up in the air during these years as the children were all actively involved in everything that they could possibly be involved in. My eldest daughter was off to high school. I had a contact at the school who helped me out with the expensive uniform that came with the private establishment. Had I not sent the children to the expensive establishment I would have ended up in Court again in another Custody battle. I figured at this point, if I just simply paid for everything that all of the attack from my ex husband, his mother and wife would go away. Famous last words…

So here I was juggling a full time position which escalated from Receptionist to Litigation Secretary at a rapid rate and 3 daughters all playing sport out of school hours, a house and day to day maintenance of all of us, as well as doing my hairdressing clients on weekends. It was busy. Generally Sundays were spent in my pyjamas washing sheets, football gear, towels and cooking a roast at the end of cleaning the entire house. All the talk of their time at the farm I used to listen to, but rarely any of it actually sunk in as I was just so busy. Different busy…when they were all babies I was busy but we could all be busy at home, now we were busy everywhere.

The girls were all growing their own little opinions of life. They were not allowed to use their phones at their father's house so they used to hide their phones and then call me secretly from the cubby house whispering. Their stepmother managed to have them offside frequently by giving her children nice fresh school lunches and mine the stale cake from weeks ago. I used to have to drive to the farm on Sunday nights, often in the fog or frost to collect the children, was not allowed to drive up the driveway so their father would drive them down with his lights on full beam just to try to irritate me…it never worked. That part I had mastered.

Whenever he would make derogatory comments about me, my car, my house, the fact I had to rent and not own my own home, I grew to laugh at him. The home one was easy. I would just say that maybe that was because he took everything and did not provide one in amongst the millions… I honestly think that it annoyed these two even more that every time they tried another legal letter, parked outside my house watching that I used to just go outside and tell them to leave. Obviously the word 'leave' may not have actually been used, but after all of these years and my children doing so well at school and in life, would one not think that they would just be supportive and stop attacking me? No…they would not.

The children's step mother used to park her car near where we lived on the hill and literally stalk me walking down the hill to work. I would turn and see her walking about 200m behind me. I could never understand the reason for this when she had driven from the farm 20 minutes away and could have parked on the other side of town closer to the highway she had to drive home on. I wished one day that the old trees in the park on the track down the hill had lower branches so I could swing and make monkey noises or something to lighten her up a bit.

Of course, my eldest daughter surprised me in her first year at high school, I had managed to get my son through school without any fights. I had taught them all that fighting was simply not acceptable…well unless they had to use self defence in an extreme situation. My eldest daughter was always the studious, quieter one of the three. One day I received a call from the school stating that she had punched a boy in the face. Excellent I thought…not! That afternoon when she came home she told me that this boy had slapped her on the bottom walking into class so I commended her on her actions, that behaviour was not acceptable and bullying is just not right. Good, we could move on from that day.

During these years there were so many funny times I could literally go on for pages. I had used the dishwasher for the first time in this house and the girls and I had a ritual of 'movie nights' where we would all get our pyjamas on and go downstairs to the living room and watch a movie with milo, chocolate, popcorn, whatever they decided on. This particular night was no exception, apart from the bubbles and soap suds all coming down the stairs and the dishwasher was leaking through the floor so it was actually raining downstairs from the kitchen. We all loved that house though, the girls loved the fact we were only 3 blocks from the city again, which, they had become accustomed to at the apartment.

Life was hectic but good. I really did not have a lot of time for the game playing events that surfaced from the farm. I did receive the washing brought into the law firm one morning by the children's stepmother. That was interesting as I was directing clients into meeting rooms and handling files for Family Law Property Settlements in Court that day. She put a large garbage bag of the children's wet clothes on the desk in Reception. She smiled sarcastically and left. I was a bit confused as to why their clothes were delivered to my place of work? Then I opened the bag. She had filled it with grass clippings from the lawn mower. My colleague and I just stared into the open bag of wet clothes all mixed with grass. I cannot repeat what my colleague said as it would not be appropriate, however, I can imagine that you would have a fair idea. My Managing Partner walked past on his way back from Court and looked in the bag. He rolled his eyes and kept walking. I think that is how everybody I was affiliated with whether it be friends, work colleagues or the like handled this behaviour. My Divorce had become quite famous in a small state actually. I had and still have so much support from so many people as to what happened to me over the years.

Chapter 20

Shared care

Obviously the grass episode was an indication that the children's stepmother was not overly excited about the Parenting Orders where they were to now have the girls for 5 days a fortnight instead of every second weekend. This incurred mixed emotions where 1, 2 or 3 of the girls intermittently would have arguments with their father and stepmother and refuse to go to the farm. I used to encourage them as it was, in legal terms, in the best interests of the children. My knowledge of Family Law grew every day so I no longer worried about any of the custody type issues and had advice on tap at any given point.

So little things like clothes coming back covered in grass were unable to be hidden from the children, particularly when they would see their mother standing outside hosing grass off clothes with a glass of wine in a business suit at night. It was clear to them now, that I did not plan to be hosing clothes so obvious where it had come from.

Their stepmother used to buy very expensive shampoo and conditioner for their ensuite. They had been given a Shetland pony at the farm so the children asked if they could wash the horse. The answer had been yes and I remember my middle daughter hiding in the cubby house calling me on her phone telling me they had lathered up the horse in a full bottle of their step mother's shampoo. I had to pretend that this was not good behaviour..that was always so difficult when, after all of the awful things they had done to me, all I wanted to do was burst out laughing.

I used to hear that the children were riding four wheel motor bikes on the farm doing 80km per hour. This, I was not happy about. I called their father and asked the question. Naturally, he denied it. I was a bit more confident and I guess had the backing of not only my Lawyer, but most of the Lawyers in the city who I used to have lunch with so I did not worry any longer, nor let these people intimidate me. So, their father bought them bike helmets, not proper safety helmets. Suddenly, I almost wished for his next stupid legal threat.

Nothing had changed in terms of clothes coming back from the farm, shoes ruined in mud, jumpers with the same holes, socks disappearing only to be noticed that the children's stepbrother I saw wearing socks that I had bought. My cap disappeared, one of my girls had lost her cap and they were off to the beach so I gave her mine for the holidays. I saw their stepmother wearing it when they dropped the children off, and one of my jumpers.

I was single and enjoying a fabulous social life in the law fraternity of the city with lunches and cocktail parties and we were finally okay financially with me working 6 or even 6.5 days a week. We would head to the beach on school holidays and also to visit my father in the seaside village that I had grown up in. Apart from the trail of legal letters that reared their head every few months, life was cruising along happily.

Sometimes, usually while watching a classic Nicholas Sparks movie, commonly known as a chick flick, and, always my favourites, I might cry in the happy ending part, which, my girls used to find hilarious but had no understanding of being alone raising children and hoping that one day I would not be totally alone, hopefully with a man who loved me, did not take all the furniture or hit me…

I would put them all to bed, even tucking them in as little teenagers and then light my candle and sit at the kitchen bench if it was cold or outside on the deck if it was warm, with my wine, looking out over the lights of the city, wondering what on earth was going to happen next. I felt as though my life was great and fun, yet part of me was just waiting for the next disaster as there was always a disaster looming. I am not even saying that in a negative way, it would just happen!

Case in question arrived. We got a dog. We already had 3 cats and 2 fish, one of which used to swim upside down but seemed happy doing that. My youngest daughter wanted a beagle. I did not really know dog breeds very well, or that beagles are not really adaptable in a confined garden in the middle of a city because they like to dig. Dig…the newest word in my life. The puppy was very cute but dug the entire back lawn right down to the pipes, ate all the neighbour's shoes outside their door, escaped and I had phone calls in the middle of talking with Family Law clients because he was running all over town. I got home one day and he was wearing my stockings off the clothes airer, had broken into the bottom door having seen one of the cats and was flying around the house after three cats. He even started to eat the weatherboards on the house. This was not working. So we had to find a home for the dog. Okay we had tried. The girls had dogs on the farm, that was enough, I was not doing this again.

Chapter 21

Spartacus

You might think this an unusual name for a chapter. I thought so too until I went back and read the Serial Killer chapter again... I am not really sure where I find these men but I have to note, and no offence to the wonderful brand of Ralph Lauren clothing but here comes another one. I can always pick them. My nights wearing bad pyjamas and socks crying in Nicholas Sparks movies were about to end...again.

Before I begin on this epic and life changing chapter for all of us, I had started talking to the girls about moving away to the mainland. I knew that I wanted to, I would have gone along time before but wanted to give the children their childhood on the farm with their father. Separating from their father I paid dearly for in my own life for what he put me through, but, I never would have taken the children away from him and his family. It would be nice if he thanked me one day but I am not holding my breath.

My father seemed now settled in the seaside village and was involved with the Bowls Club and had numerous friends and a social calendar far outwaying anybody my age or younger, so, I felt that if the girls were keen to move, that perhaps before they finished school might be the right time. My father was always a part of our lives and I would need to make sure that he was going to be okay if we did leave the state. The girls were now of the age that they could choose their time with each parent and I had always left that option open incase they had decided they wanted to go and live more of the time with their father, but they had never requested that. Possibly the stale cake out there...who knows?

In amongst these chats we attended my brother's wedding on the coast. There was one morning I was standing on the balcony of the hotel we were staying at looking at the sunrise over the beach when my eldest daughter came out and said, "Mum, why don't we move up here?"

It was the state that 2 of them were born in, it had a great climate, great prospects for their future, my father and late mother had loved their years there….. thoughts started to flood into my mind of the possibilities.

Time proceeded and that is exactly what it became, thoughts. I started messaging a man that I had gone to school with, who, ironically lived on the coast now. I never liked him at school, always thought he was 'up himself' to be honest. He became very chatty on Facebook and I would spend my evenings after the children went to bed talking to this man.

Enter Spartacus.

It all happened rather quickly and I felt all wrapped up in the charming compliments and attention. It is really amazing how an educated and, I would like to think, respectable and intelligent girl can warn friends and advise on relationships yet when it comes to yourself, turn to mush and fall for complete and utter self centred control freaks. This one, no exception. On his potential third marriage prospect as well. Everybody is entitled to marry as many times as you like, however, when the weddings start to take over the relationship tries I do feel that perhaps slowing down and seeing if the relationship will work first can often, but not always, be a good idea.

So, into this relationship full force was he. I went along with it, receiving flowers at work, lovely messages and all of the Nicholas Sparks type dreams for any girl. I flew to the coast, he flew to the island, I flew my children up for a holiday at the beach to meet his children and before long we were packing up our cottage to move. The girls were excited to be moving away. I explained to their father that if they came down for all school holidays that he would actually have more time with them than with us living 20 minutes away. He agreed. No…. surely this was too good to be true?

Was I right? Was their father predictable? Yes.

And then I was served at work…Relocation Order Application. Off we all went to Court again. Unbelievable. He would not buy them a pair of $7 sport socks but would spend another few thousand on taking me to Court …again!

So part of the conditions of me being able to take the girls to live in another state, according to their father was that I had to have a job organised, a private school organised and a house. I think he might have thought that would stop me. Really, he should have known by now that I was not one to give up. My daughters were keen as mustard to move as it was a great big adventure and my son was already living away so I just got to organising as per these Court

Orders. I do still know that I can thank Spartacus for his part he played in making this all possible and a lot easier than if I had had to organise everything alone.

Spartacus went and found us a mansion on the river, pool, boatdeck, huge yard, palm trees, loads of bedrooms for his children as well. It was nothing like what we had ever had. The children were excited and I was starting in my blurred vision to think that maybe this man was the infamous 'one'…

The children's father had to have the girls full time while I spent 4 weeks putting all of his Court requests in order. He told me that he did not want them full time so I just explained that he would have to as he was the person who had created the Court Orders and that maybe he should have thought about that before making this as difficult as possible for me.

It was the longest 4 weeks of my life, that and I had a stupid phone plan so the calls cost be nearly $3000 for 30 days talking to the girls every night. But I managed to start a job in a law firm up here, move into the mansion with Spartacus and organise a lovely school for the girls. Then I received a phone call from my ex husband right in the middle of the workday. He told me that I had to fly the children up that afternoon, that he did not want them there any longer and that they had upset his wife…that part I was not surprised about. The few thousand dollars on his precious Court Orders suddenly went out the window as he breached his own Orders…

We flew the girls up that night, they arrived in their school dresses with huge bags of clothes, not folded, thrown in with football boots covered in mud, no grass this time ironically, just mud. The poor little darlings looked like starved homeless children who needed their hair washed. I had made their favourite dinner and they were so hungry and excited to be at our new home. They were quite shocked as they had gone to school that morning only to be pulled out before lunchtime and taken to the Headmaster's Office and told that they were being taken to the airport by their father earlier than they thought. What a day, the poor little girls did not even have the chance to say goodbye to their friends or pack up their books. I was liasing with the Headmaster the entire time and he was happy they were being shipped up to me.

We had some time there on the river, a bit over a year from memory. The name Spartacus you must be wondering… well this charmer did not do the really nasty Domestic Violence of the other yoyos I had gone out with. I believe this was more damaging really. I was spoilt with flowers and gifts and then told to grow my hair, cut my hair, lose weight, put on weight, wear more dresses…usual controlling behaviour. Because of my past experiences I just went along with it. I fell back in the TRAP. He would actually walk around the house saying to all of the children including his own, that he was Spartacus. At first I thought he was joking but then he was so overly confident in himself that I thought he did actually think he was some sort of superhero or something. He even sat the 5 of them down and made them watch the movie. Oh dear. There was no mansion on the face of the earth worth dealing with this…

Of course the girls were all very much teenagers, we had learner licence books and closed bedroom doors, makeup stuck to the carpet, selfies, dance sessions all dressed up, movies made on the pontoon. It was all happening under our roof.

I was spoilt some of the time. I would be told which dress to wear and which necklace, taken out to dinner whereby he would always walk in front of me, not next to me, sometimes I would nearly be running to keep up. The Serial Killer used to do that too. Girls, be very aware of the man who always marches off in front of you, never guiding his girl through a door like a true gentleman. I think I had taken narcissist to a whole new level. I was able to stop working for a while whilst with Spartacus, because he really did not like me working in an office with male Lawyers.

I enrolled at Law School and studied a full time load of subjects. It distracted me from him really. He never stopped talking. He told me I could become the Lawyer and he could run my office and wear shorts and go for coffees in his black range rover…I just looked at him feeling my eyebrow uncontrollably move up in disbelief.

I still to this day not hate Spartacus, he only hit me once, drugged me once at a function and basically caused me to drink too much because he did, we were just really not suited. I did let him propose on an island beach, no ring…down on one knee trying to do everything right except he had only brought one champagne glass for himself not one for me…classic. We were engaged for a year, then I left him. I threw the ring out into the ocean so I am hoping that a lucky fish is wearing it. His next girlfriend was engaged quickly too, she went. He has a new one apparently who is also wearing a ring. Habits stick they say.

I held no emotion leaving the mansion. It was just a relief to not have to drink wine all night listening to him and watching him smoke a whole packet of cigarettes in about 2 hours, then wake up to him doing weights at 5:00am in front of the bed telling me how good he looked. I still think he was on speed or something, no one can have that much energy after 15 beers and a bottle of red wine 6 hours earlier. He exhausted me. I found solace in doing my assignments in the middle of the night, see..let it go! A tactic that has been my saving grace.

We packed up and left the mansion. The girls were all excited about our next adventure… in a tiny two bedroom unit with Police presence most nights…a total turn around from the posh mansion on the river, however, it was what I could afford in rent.

Chapter 22
The Block

I found us a little two bedroom unit right across the road from the beach. Massive downsize this was from the mansion, but, to be fair, a lot more the size of some of our previous houses. I was excited that it would not take me 5 hours to clean, that in itself is worth a break up! The Block..really was like a caption from the land before time or some kind of ridiculous chaos that became our home. There were 8 units, old style, your car parked at the door. I walked up the driveway the day I had a look at Unit 6. A bubbly girl bounced out into the driveway with a Jim Beam can and cigarette, "and who the f★★k are you?" I jumped at first and said that my girls and I were moving into Unit 6. So here we were. There was a maori girl next door with her daughter and they are great friends today. There was a girl on the other side of me who used to scream at her daughter all the time, there were brazillians over the fence who used to party and sing all night. The Police were generally at another of the units a few nights a week as that couple used to fight all the time.

And then there was us, my girls all leaving for school with their beautifully brushed hair and navy blue ribbons. We soon blended into the scene of the Block. I went next door for wines and managed to fall through my neighbour's table with her cousin from New Zealand while dancing. I think I relaxed and let my hair down a bit there! My eldest daughter was of the age to go out and came home in an ambulance after one too many vodka shots. Suddenly we were accepted and those days were possibly some of the funniest memories. I had a lot of support in that first 6 months there, got a job out of one of the tenants and life started to become quiet and normal again. My eldest daughter decided to move out and so it was just the two younger daughters and myself.

We were at the beach. To be honest, I have never really left the beach since. I have moved to a few different places but, after living at the Block, always gravitate back to the beach. There is something special about hearing the ocean at night, it is like a meditation without meditating. It centres your soul I am sure. It is notoriously cooler and often windy, your windows are always covered in salt and things magically rust.

Our doors never locked properly because the locks were filled with salt, however, no one came near the Block anyway because the Police were there so often, it felt like the safest place in the world. There was always someone home and we all looked out for each other. We never locked our doors, tried that once and we had to push my youngest daughter up onto the top balcony to get in. From that day we just went out and left the doors open. I used to wander over the road to the beach without shoes at any given time of the day. There was a wooden bridge going across from the park and then the open ocean beach, tranquil some days, rough on others.

I found peace at the Block. I built my garden of frangipanis and used to sit outside at night still after my girls had gone to bed with my candle and wine listening to the ocean and staring at the stars. I felt close to my late mother here as she had loved the coast. Some nights my neighbour would pop her head over my fence and say "nightcap?" We would both sit and chat and stare up at the stars. We shared stories of our lives, breakups, ex husbands, children. It was obviously meant to be that I was in those surroundings and not alone so I could heal. I did not go out or anything, even though my neighbours and their relatives visiting would invite me. I just needed time to myself to heal really.

I kept up with the school routine and had a lot of the girl's friend's stay on Wednesday nights for football. I think I might have been the parent who gave a couple of them their first champagne and also listened to a few pregnancy scares. They were all growing up so fast. My middle daughter was House Captain so in amongst all the moves, the single mother turmoil of these 4 children's lives, I obviously did something right as they were passing school and doing really well at sport.

I had another couple of jobs that did not work out, it was different to the law firm on the island, up here you are not known, it is a lot more cut throat in some sectors and I miraculously fell into every awful office or salon or any kind of employment and hated most jobs I had up here! I just figured that one day I would find the right one?! I managed to keep food on the table and school fees paid. I really have no idea how I paid the school fees on top of everything else all those years but I did!

But we were all happy at the beach. We never wore shoes much, adapted to that beach lifestyle perfectly. I loved being able to just walk across the road onto the beach without having to drive anywhere or put shoes on.

Sometimes my maori neighbour and I would take a glass of wine across the road at night and just sit in the sand listening to the ocean and have a catch up chat. This was normally when my girls were doing homework which often ended up with them dancing or singing to music and generally laughing, wrestling and occasionally a full taekwondo sparring event in their bedroom while my neighbour's daughter would be cheering the All Blacks rugby finals so loudly that we would opt for peace and quiet and go over the road to the beach.

The Coast beaches are amazing at all times, I do not like them when it is busy with tourists in the middle of the day but the best time is early in the morning walking or at night when there are barely any people and it is so peaceful with the only sound being the waves crashing. We had one interesting night when my middle daughter was on her Learners Licence...the neighbours had had a barbeque over in the park this particular day and we had all had a few wines. Our black cat would still wander. This time he had wandered up to the next suburb so I suggested to my middle daughter that she drive so we could pick him up. He wore a tag still so people would call me from wherever he would wander to. I thought this should be okay as I was not driving after the barbeque...until my daughter forgot to turn the car headlights on so we were pulled over. Naturally I was breathalysed for alcohol and blew over the limit being the 'responsible' parent in the passenger seat. Oh dear...well we had the ride in the Police car, both wearing our pyjamas and the cat sitting in the middle of the back seat of the Police car. He already knew most of the Police as he used to go and visit them at the station.

Licence gone for me. Yes, another spectacular disaster. My daughters were quite excited as they could then drive my car to school each day. Our cat wandered everywhere still, he went on the tram one day. He went on stage at the Convention Centre, had his own food bowl at the Meriton Hotel, was often dropped home in taxis, he was such a character!

So the block days were meant to be a part of this story, potentially a bigger part than I thought.

Chapter 23

The Marathon Runner

I can tell what you are all thinking already... NO! Not another one...

Well I have to say that I really did not see this one coming. I certainly was not looking for a man. I think I was just enjoying being single, no more attacks from the children's father and apart from some terrible jobs, life was going quite well. But alas, we can still be weak and fall at times. My eldest daughter left school, middle daughter about to, we had hit the formal years and graduations and surprisingly had all survived! The girls were all happy and had good friendships.

So, my neighbour's family used to visit often and I had got to know quite a few of them, there were quite a few! They were all going up to the local pub one night, along with the little bubbly neighbour. They came over and told me to put on a dress and come. I said no. My girls were not even home as they were off with friends and had the car and sleepover nights going on as teenagers do.

My neighbour told me I was too quiet and I had been here 6 months and not gone anywhere socially and to put a dress on. So, I did. I found a little black dress in the back of my cupboard and tossed my hair up as it was half full of salt and sand from being at the beach in the wind, put some lip gloss on and some flat white sandals. I did not fuss with makeup apart from the usual mascara and was not really in the right mood to be heading out, basically had not made that much effort but figured I would just have fun and it was only a couple of blocks up the road so I felt quite comfortable going. I had heard that Spartacus had already moved on with his next to be fiancé so knew that I would not run into him.

Well, I think it was the 'let the hair down' night. We all played pool and drank loads of champagne and laughed and had a fun time. There was a band there and I just felt alive again. I was happy having all the months alone and had grown my garden and my girls were happy. I was not looking for anything to complicate any of that. I was not looking at any of the males at the bar. A few tried talking to me and I just avoided them as I was just feeling free!

Then he walked past me. I was talking to his friend. I remember watching him ordering a drink. At this point I knew that my judgment was a little blurred after so many champagnes but I looked at him …

My Mother had always said to look at their shoes. I was not sure what that actually meant, but thinking back, when I first went out with the children's father he was wearing what I call 'bank' shoes, the pale grey type. I never liked those shoes. My mother had explained that that was a sign we were not going to be together forever because I had not liked his shoes.

This man had normal looking black lace up shoes, denim jeans, a black t-shirt, normal mousy coloured hair and a nice smile. He was tallish, slender build and did not appear too overly confident, or arrogant, or march in front of people. I deliberately walked past him and brushed my hand against his, he noticed. Why did I do that? Okay so I did…hoping that I would not regret doing so!

We talked and then he and his friends were going to the casino, I had managed to lose my friends so decided I could go along too as this was my first night out for ages! I felt safe enough as it was a group of people and the streets were busy. The casino was also only about 3 blocks from our unit and with the Police station in between.

We danced at the casino and he kissed me on the dancefloor. It was quite a romantic kiss. We ended up sitting over on the beach at about 4am. He walked me home and I said goodbye. There was something about him that got me…well my interest I guess.

To be honest, I thought nothing of the whole night, other than it made me think, once again, after being hurt, that maybe there is a nice man out there for me… and that was that. It was a wonderful night and it was over.

I sat outside during that week with my neighbour and she asked me about that night. I could not remember his name. Well, that did not look very good but then I thought well, I was not going to see him again so who cares? I said to her that I liked him, he seemed different..gentle, not aggressive or arrogant or overly confident. His face crossed my mind during that week but I basically filed those thoughts away. She asked if I had given him my number. I said no. I said that I had given him my email address though. He had said that he was a marathon runner so immediately I was trying hard to remove him from my mind as I was not a runner so figured that we would not work.

Days went on and I did not hear from this mysterious marathon man so I just got on with life again. I was notoriously destined to have nothing but disasters with men so I put all thoughts away in the 'too hard basket'.

Then a couple of days later my neighbour knocked at my open door, because it actually would not shut either now as well as lock. She said, "There is a letter in my mailbox for you". It was funny as I had mail with the same handwritten name on the front that I had not opened yet. So we ran down to the mailboxes…And, the same letter had been put in all the boxes of the 8 units in the block… Everyone thought it pretty cute that he knew where I lived but not the actual unit so had written to me in every mailbox. At least he had remembered my name, unlike me. But every other man I had been obsessed with being available and knowing their details yet this time it was different, I was oblivious to the attention. It is commonly known that someone can appear in your life when you least expect it, I wonder if this was him?

I have to say that all the printed letters in the mailboxes is possibly one of the cutest and most romantic gestures of which I had heard…

Was this the infamous Mr Right? Was this my Man from Snowy River ideal in disguise as a marathon runner? I guess that is a story for another day.

~~~~~~

Printed in the United States
By Bookmasters